The Official Rails-to-Trails
Conservancy Guidebook

Rail-Trails

Southern
New England

The definitive guide to multiuse trails in Connecticut,
Massachusetts, and Rhode Island

T0160448

WILDERNESS PRESS ... *on the trail since 1967*

Rail-Trails: Southern New England
1st Edition, 6th printing 2021
Copyright © 2018 by Rails-to-Trails Conservancy

Cover and interior photographs copyright © 2018 by Rails-to-Trails Conservancy
Maps: Lohnes+Wright; map data courtesy of Environmental Systems Research Institute
Cover design: Scott McGrew
Book design: Annie Long

Library of Congress Cataloging-in-Publication Data

Names: Rails-to-Trails Conservancy, issuing body.
Title: The official Rails-to-Trails Conservancy guidebook. Rail-trails Southern New
  England : the definitive guide to multiuse trails in Connecticut, Massachusetts, and
  Rhode Island.
Other titles: Rail-trails Southern New England
Description: 1st edition. | Birmingham, AL : Wilderness Press, 2018. | Includes index.
Identifiers: LCCN 2017053341| ISBN 9780899978994 (pbk.) | ISBN
  9780899979007 (ebk.)
Subjects: LCSH: Rail-trails—Connecticut—Guidebooks. | Outdoor recreation—
  Connecticut—Guidebooks. | Rail-trails—Massachusetts—Guidebooks. | Out-
  door recreation—Massachusetts—Guidebooks. | Rail-trails—Rhode Island—Guidebooks.
  | Outdoor recreation—Rhode Island—Guidebooks. | Connecticut—Guidebooks. |
  Massachusetts—Guidebooks. | Rhode Island—Guidebooks.
Classification: LCC GV191.42.C8 O44 2018 | DDC 796.50974—dc23
LC record available at https://lccn.loc.gov/2017053341

Manufactured in China

Published by: **WILDERNESS PRESS**
An imprint of AdventureKEEN
2204 First Ave. S, Ste. 102
Birmingham, AL 35233
800-678-7008; fax (877) 374-9016

Visit wildernesspress.com for a complete listing of our books and for ordering information. Contact us at our website, at facebook.com/wildernesspress1967, or at twitter.com
/wilderness1967 with questions or comments. To find out more about who we are and
what we're doing, visit blog.wildernesspress.com.

Distributed by Publishers Group West

Front cover: Vernon Rails-to-Trails (see page 54), photographed by Angela Mips; *back
cover:* Reformatory Branch Trail (see page 157), photographed by Aykut Bilge

SAFETY NOTICE: Although Wilderness Press and Rails-to-Trails Conservancy have
made every attempt to ensure that the information in this book is accurate at press time,
they are not responsible for any loss, damage, injury, or inconvenience that may occur to
anyone while using this book. You are responsible for your own safety and health while in
the wilderness. The fact that a trail is described in this book does not mean that it will be
safe for you. Be aware that trail conditions can change from day to day. Always check local
conditions, know your own limitations, and consult a map.

About Rails-to-Trails Conservancy

Headquartered in Washington, D.C., Rails-to-Trails Conservancy (RTC) is a nonprofit organization dedicated to creating a nationwide network of trails from former rail lines and connecting corridors to build healthier places for healthier people.

Railways helped build America. Spanning from coast to coast, these ribbons of steel linked people, communities, and enterprises, spurring commerce and forging a single nation that bridges a continent. But in recent decades, many of these routes have fallen into disuse, severing communal ties that helped bind Americans together.

When RTC opened its doors in 1986, the rail-trail movement was in its infancy. Most projects focused on single, linear routes in rural areas, created for recreation and conservation. RTC sought broader protection for the unused corridors, incorporating rural, suburban, and urban routes.

Year after year, RTC's efforts to protect and align public funding with trail building created an environment that allowed trail advocates in communities across the country to initiate trail projects. These ever-growing ranks of trail professionals, volunteers, and RTC supporters have built momentum for the national rail-trails movement. As the number of supporters multiplied, so did the rail-trails.

Americans now enjoy more than 23,000 miles of open rail-trails, and as they flock to the trails to connect with family members and friends, enjoy nature, and get to places in their local neighborhoods and beyond, their economic prosperity, health, and overall well-being continue to flourish.

A signature endeavor of RTC is **TrailLink.com,** America's portal to these rail-trails, as well as other multiuse trails. When RTC launched TrailLink.com in 2000, our organization was one of the first to compile such detailed trail information on a national scale. Today, the website continues to play a critical role in both encouraging and satisfying the country's growing need for opportunities to ride, walk, skate, or run for recreation or transportation. This free trail-finder database—which includes detailed descriptions, interactive maps, photo galleries, and firsthand ratings and reviews—can be used as a companion resource to the trails in this guidebook.

The national voice for more than 160,000 members and supporters, RTC is committed to ensuring a better future for America made possible by trails and the connections they inspire. Learn more at **railstotrails.org.**

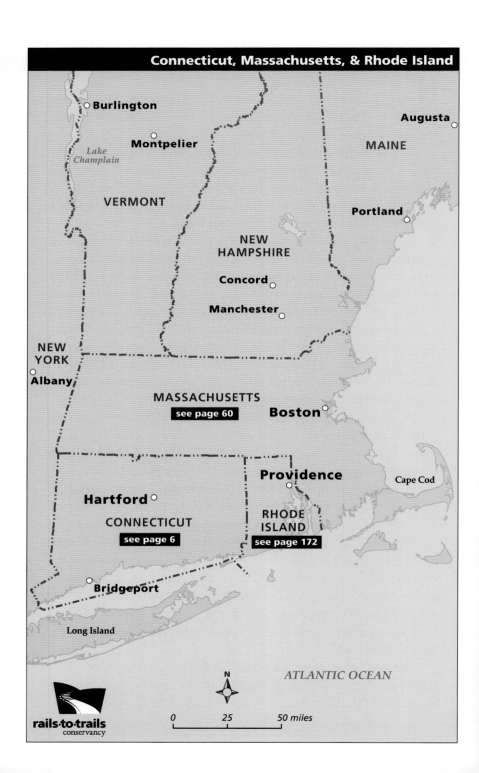

Table of Contents

CONNECTICUT 6

MASSACHUSETTS 60

Connecticut's Farmington Canal Heritage Trail (see page 19)

RHODE ISLAND 172

Foreword

For those of you who have already experienced the sheer enjoyment and freedom of riding on a rail-trail, welcome back! You'll find *Rail-Trails: Southern New England* to be a useful and fun guide to your favorite trails, as well as an introduction to pathways you have yet to travel.

For readers who are discovering for the first time the adventures possible on a rail-trail, thank you for joining the rail-trail movement. Since 1986, Rails-to-Trails Conservancy has been the leading supporter and defender of these priceless public corridors. We are excited to bring you *Rail-Trails: Southern New England,* so you too can enjoy some of the region's premier rail-trails and multiuse trails. These hiking and biking trails are ideal ways to connect with your community, with nature, and with your friends and family.

I've found that trails have a way of bringing people together, and as you'll see from this book, you have opportunities in every state you visit to get on a great trail. Whether you're looking for a place to exercise, explore, commute, or play, there is a trail in this book for you.

So I invite you to sit back, relax, pick a trail that piques your interest—and then get out, get active, and have some fun. I'll be out on the trails too, so be sure to wave as you go by.

Happy trails,

Keith Laughlin, President
Rails-to-Trails Conservancy

Acknowledgments

Special thanks to Gene Bisbee and Amy Ahn for their work on this book. We are also appreciative of the following contributors and to all the trail managers we called on for assistance to ensure the maps, photographs, and trail descriptions are as accurate as possible.

Milo Bateman

Jim Brown

Ken Bryan

Ryan Cree

Cindy Dickerson

Eli Griffen

Avery Harmon

Yvonne Mwangi

Jimmy O'Connor

Kenneth Rusk

Anya Saretzky

Liz Sewell

Tom Sexton

Leeann Sinpatanasakul

Laura Stark

Scott Stark

Derek Strout

The Norwottuck Branch of the Mass Central Rail Trail (see page 118)

Introduction

Rail-Trails: Southern New England highlights 52 of the top rail-trails and other multiuse pathways in Connecticut, Massachusetts, and Rhode Island. These trails offer a broad range of experiences to suit nearly every taste, from vibrant cities to remote forests, from sweeping coastal vistas to narrow wooded ravines, and from challenging mountain biking adventures to relaxing waterfront strolls.

Within these pages, you'll find lengthy trails for multiday journeys, including Connecticut's Air Line State Park Trail and Massachusetts's Mass Central Rail Trail, as well as short but sweet options, such as the beautiful Bridge of Flowers and the Vernon Rails-to-Trails, which is featured on our cover.

A standout is Cape Cod's Shining Sea Bikeway, which was named after the lyrics to "America the Beautiful" and championed by Barbara Burwell, whose work on the rail-trail project inspired her son David Burwell. He cofounded Rails-to-Trails Conservancy (RTC) and became a visionary leader of the rails-to-trails movement. America now has more than 2,000 rail-trails, and they can be found in all 50 states.

Two exemplary rail-trails in this book have been inducted into RTC's Hall of Fame: Massachusetts's Minuteman Bikeway and Rhode Island's East Bay Bike Path. The Minuteman Bikeway, spanning 10 miles through Boston's northwest suburbs, roughly traces Paul Revere's midnight ride in April 1775 to warn local militias about advancing British troops. The East Bay Bike Path offers spectacular maritime views on its 14-mile run from Providence to Bristol.

Several trails in this region are being stitched together in the developing East Coast Greenway (ECG), which aims to link trails across 15 states, from Maine to Florida. You'll find many ECG-designated pathways in this book, including the Farmington Canal Heritage Trail, a north-south route that nearly spans Connecticut, and the Charles River Bike Path, dotted with fantastic museums and parks on its course from Boston to the city's western suburbs.

No matter which routes in Rail-Trails: Southern New England you choose, you'll experience the unique history, culture, and geography of each, as well as the communities that have built and embraced them.

What Is a Rail-Trail?

Rail-trails are multiuse public paths built along former railroad corridors. Most often flat or following a gentle grade, they are suited to walking, running, cycling, mountain biking, in-line skating, cross-country skiing, horseback

OPPOSITE: *The Massachusetts section of the Blackstone River Greenway (see page 174)*

riding, and wheelchair use. Since the 1960s, Americans have created more than 23,000 miles of rail-trails throughout the country.

These extremely popular recreation and transportation corridors traverse urban, suburban, and rural landscapes. Many preserve historical landmarks, while others serve as wildlife conservation corridors, linking isolated parks and establishing greenways in developed areas. Rail-trails also stimulate local economies by boosting tourism and promoting trailside businesses.

What Is a Rail-with-Trail?

A rail-with-trail is a public path that parallels a still-active rail line. Some run adjacent to high-speed, scheduled trains, often linking public transportation stations, while others follow tourist routes and slow-moving excursion trains. Many share an easement, separated from the rails by extensive fencing. More than 275 rails-with-trails exist in the United States.

What Is the Rail-Trail Hall of Fame?

In 2007 RTC began recognizing exemplary rail-trails around the country through its Rail-Trail Hall of Fame. Inductees are selected based on such merits as scenic value, high use, trail and trailside amenities, historical significance, excellence in management and maintenance of facility, community connections, and geographic distribution. These iconic rail-trails, which have been singled out from more than 2,000 in the United States, have earned RTC's highest honor and represent tangible realizations of our vision to create a more walkable, bikeable, healthier America. Hall of Fame rail-trails are indicated in this book with a special blue icon; for the full list of Hall of Fame rail-trails, visit **railstotrails.org/halloffame.**

Rail-Trails: Southern New England provides the information you'll need to plan a rewarding trek. With words to inspire you and maps to chart your path, it makes choosing the best route a breeze. Following are some of the highlights.

Maps

You'll find three levels of maps in this book: an **overall regional map, state locator maps**, and **detailed trail maps**.

The trails in this book are located in Connecticut, Massachusetts, and Rhode Island. Each chapter details a particular state's network of trails, marked on a locator map at the beginning of the chapter. Use these maps to find the trails nearest you, or select several neighboring trails and plan a weekend hiking or biking excursion. Once you find a trail on a state locator map, simply flip to the corresponding number for a full description. Accompanying trail maps mark each route's access roads, trailheads, parking areas, restrooms, and other defining features.

Key to Map Icons

Parking

Drinking
Water

Restrooms

Featured
Trail

Connecting
Trail

Active
Railroad

Trail Descriptions

Trails are listed in alphabetical order within each chapter. Each description leads with a set of summary information, including trail endpoints and mileage, a roughness index, the trail surface, and possible uses.

The map and summary information list the trail endpoints (either a city, street, or more specific location), with suggested points from which to start and finish. Additional access points are marked on the maps and mentioned in the trail descriptions. The maps and descriptions also highlight available amenities, including parking and restrooms, as well as such area attractions as shops, services, museums, parks, and stadiums. Trail length is listed in miles.

Each trail bears a **roughness index** rating from 1 to 3. A rating of 1 indicates a smooth, level surface that is accessible to users of all ages and abilities. A 2 rating means the surface may be loose and/or uneven and could pose a problem for road bikes and wheelchairs. A 3 rating suggests a rough surface that is only recommended for mountain bikers and hikers. Surfaces can range from asphalt or concrete to ballast, boardwalk, cinder, crushed stone, gravel, grass, dirt, sand, and/or wood chips. Where relevant, trail descriptions address alternating surface conditions.

All trails are open to pedestrians, and most allow bicycles, except where noted in the trail summary or description. The summary also indicates wheelchair access. Other possible uses include in-line skating, mountain biking, horseback riding, fishing, and cross-country skiing. While most trails are off-limits to motor vehicles, some local trail organizations do allow all-terrain vehicles and snowmobiles.

Trail descriptions suggest an ideal itinerary for each route, including the best parking areas and access points, where to begin, your direction of travel, and any highlights along the way. Following each description are directions to the recommended trailheads.

Each trail description also lists a local website for further information. Be sure to visit these websites in advance for updates and current conditions. **TrailLink.com** is another great resource for updated content on the trails in this guidebook.

Trail Use

Rail-trails are popular destinations for a range of users, often making them busy places to enjoy the outdoors. Following basic trail etiquette and safety guidelines will make your experience more pleasant.

➤ **Keep to the right,** except when passing.

➤ **Pass on the left,** and give a clear audible warning: "Passing on your left."

➤ **Be aware** of other trail users, particularly around corners and blind spots, and be especially careful when entering a trail, changing direction, or passing, so that you don't collide with traffic.

➤ **Respect wildlife** and public and private property; leave no trace and take out litter.

➤ **Control your speed,** especially near pedestrians, playgrounds, and heavily congested areas.

➤ **Travel single file.** Cyclists and pedestrians should ride or walk single file in congested areas or areas with reduced visibility.

➤ **Cross carefully** at intersections; always look both ways and yield to through traffic. Pedestrians have the right-of-way.

➤ **Keep one ear open and volume low** on portable listening devices to increase your awareness of your surroundings.

➤ **Wear a helmet** and other safety gear if you're cycling or in-line skating.

➤ **Consider visibility.** Wear reflective clothing, use bicycle lights, or bring flashlights or helmet-mounted lights for tunnel passages or twilight excursions.

➤ **Keep moving,** and don't block the trail. When taking a rest, turn off the trail to the right. Groups should avoid congregating on or blocking the trails. If you have an accident on the trail, move to the right as soon as possible.

➤ **Bicyclists yield** to all other trail users. Pedestrians yield to horses. If in doubt, yield to all other trail users.

➤ **Dogs are permitted** on most trails, but **some trails through parks, wildlife refuges, or other sensitive areas may not allow pets;** it's best to check the trail website before your visit. If pets are permitted, keep your dog on a short leash and under your control at all times. Remove dog waste in a designated trash receptacle.

➤ **Teach your children** these trail essentials, and be especially diligent to keep them out of faster-moving trail traffic.

➤ **Be prepared,** especially on long-distance rural trails. Bring water, snacks, maps, a light source, matches, and other equipment you may need. Because some areas may not have good reception for cell phones, know where you're going, and tell someone else your plan.

Key to Trail Use

| walking | cycling | wheelchair access | in-line skating | mountain biking |

| fishing | horseback riding | cross-country skiing | snowmobiling |

Learn More

To learn about additional multiuse trails in your area or to plan a trip to an area beyond the scope of this book, visit Rails-to-Trails Conservancy's trailfinder website **TrailLink.com,** a free resource with more than 32,000 miles of mapped rail-trails and multiuse trails nationwide.

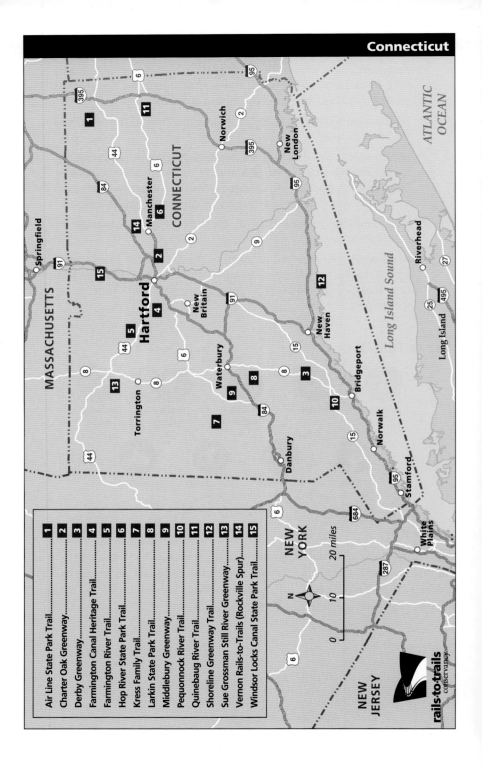

Connecticut

Air Line State Park Trail...... **1**
Charter Oak Greenway........ **2**
Derby Greenway................. **3**
Farmington Canal Heritage Trail.... **4**
Farmington River Trail......... **5**
Hop River State Park Trail.... **6**
Kress Family Trail.............. **7**
Larkin State Park Trail........ **8**
Middlebury Greenway......... **9**
Pequonnock River Trail....... **10**
Quinebaug River Trail......... **11**
Shoreline Greenway Trail..... **12**
Sue Grossman Still River Greenway.... **13**
Vernon Rails-to-Trails (Rockville Spur)...... **14**
Windsor Locks Canal State Park Trail...... **15**

Connecticut

A bridge over the Shepaug River on the Kress Family Trail (see page 29)

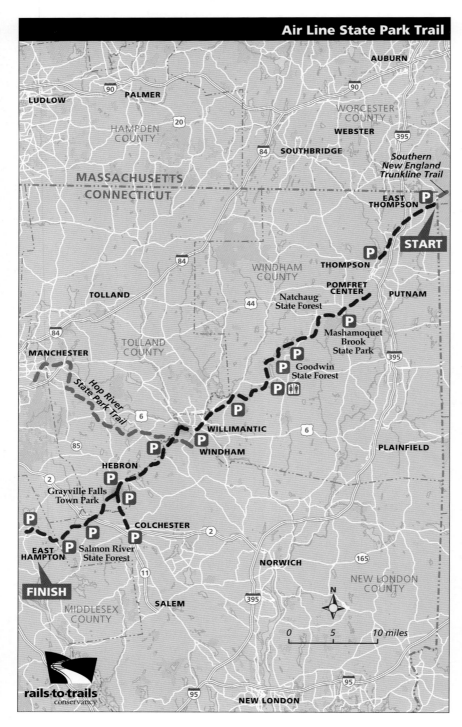

The Air Line State Park Trail winds nearly 55 miles from the northeast corner of Connecticut, where the state borders Massachusetts, down to East Hampton in the heart of the state. The pathway is nearly seamless, with only one major gap through Putnam. Over the state border, you can make a contiguous connection to the Southern New England Trunkline Trail, which heads more than 20 miles east to Franklin, Massachusetts.

The rail-trail showcases the engineering behind the Air Line Railroad, laid down through this hilly region in 1873 as part of a direct route between Boston and New York. As the railroad's name implies, the tracks ran flat and straight, like a line in the air. The Air Line employed the finest trains of the day, featuring the Pullman Palace Car, marketed as the White Train for its luxurious white-and-gold decor.

Numerous bridges enhance the trail experience.

Counties
Middlesex, New London, Tolland, Windham

Endpoints
CT–MA state line near E. Thompson Road, 0.7 mile east of New Road (East Thompson), to Riverside Dr. and Old Route 12 (Thompson); and Averill St. and Railroad St. (Pomfret Center) to Main St. between Summit St. and Walnut Ave. (East Hampton)

Mileage
54.6

Type
Rail-Trail

Roughness Index
2–3

Surfaces
Ballast, Dirt, Gravel

At this juncture in Willimantic, the Air Line State Park Trail meets the Hop River State Park Trail.

Northern Section: East Thompson to Thompson

If you begin your adventure on the trail's northern end, note that parking is not available at the tip. Instead, find parking 0.5 mile farther at the intersection of New Road and Thompson Road in East Thompson. From there, you'll head southwest on the trail. The trail feels completely secluded, as it has few entry points and no view of the roads or sound of traffic for miles.

A word of caution about the trail's surface, however: The original ballast covers this 6-mile northern section and it becomes bumpy and rocky at various points. Riders often have to dismount due to the uneven nature of the ballast, so a fat-tire bicycle is highly recommended. The trail ends in the southern outskirts of Thompson, near the border of neighboring Putnam.

A gap of 7.5 miles lies between the northern and southern sections of the Air Line State Park Trail. Pick up the pathway again at the intersection of Averill Street and Railroad Street in Pomfret Center, a small village nestled within the larger Pomfret, one of the oldest towns in the state with its incorporation in 1713.

Southern Section: Pomfret Center to East Hampton

From Pomfret Center, you'll follow the pathway just over 19 miles southwest to Willimantic, skirting Mashamoquet Brook State Park, Natchaug State Forest, and Goodwin State Forest, which offer numerous recreational options such as hiking and equestrian trails, camping, and wildlife viewing.

When you arrive in downtown Willimantic, you'll find that the trail ends at Jillson Square Park, but with a short bit of on-road riding, you can pick up the trail again just south of the intersection of Bridge Street and Riverside Drive. Traveling west along the Willimantic River, you'll see the Connecticut Eastern Railroad Museum in 0.8 mile. For history buffs, its vintage locomotives and railroad buildings are well worth a visit. The museum is also adjacent to a juncture with the Hop River State Park Trail (see page 26), a scenic route heading 20 miles northwest to

Manchester. Both trails are part of the East Coast Greenway, which will connect communities along the Eastern seaboard from Maine to Florida.

Heading southwest down the trail, you'll arrive at a fork in Hebron after 8.3 miles. Keep right to stay on the main Air Line State Park Trail; the other option is a 3.5-mile spur to Colchester. Though the trail is primarily dirt here, this section offers many attractions that make it worthwhile. From the fork, it's 1.4 miles to beautiful Grayville Falls Town Park, which offers waterfalls and wooded hikes. Nature abounds as you continue along the corridor, and you'll have access to Raymond Brook Marsh and Salmon River State Forest.

Numerous bridges offer lovely views, including the Blackledge and Jeremy River crossings. When you reach the Bunk Hill Road trailhead parking, you can take an on-road side excursion of 1.4 miles to reach the Comstock Covered Bridge. Originally built in 1791, it's one of the last remaining historical covered bridges in the state.

From the Bunk Hill trailhead, you're only 3.6 miles from trail's end, but there's still more to see. You'll cross the Rapallo and Lyman Viaducts, which were originally built in the 1870s and offer stunning views of the surrounding hills and forests. The trail ends in East Hampton, once known as Bell Town for the 30 bell-making companies that settled here.

CONTACT: www.ct.gov/deep/airlinetrail

DIRECTIONS

With such a long trail, there are numerous parking locations. Below are a few options; use the link above or **TrailLink.com** to find others.

To reach the northernmost parking area, take I-395 to Exit 50, and head east on CT 200. In 0.6 mile, turn left onto CT 193 N, and go 1.6 miles. Turn right onto E. Thompson Road, and go 3.1 miles. Parking is available at the trailhead near the intersection of New Road and E. Thompson Road.

To reach trailhead parking in Pomfret, take US 44 to Pomfret (about 40 miles east of Hartford), and turn north to remain on US 44. In 0.6 mile turn left onto Railroad St., then immediately take a right onto Averill St. The trail parking lot is on your left.

To reach the Air Line State Park Trail in Willimantic, take I-384 to US 6, and continue east on US 6 for 10.8 miles. Continue straight onto CT 66, and go 1.9 miles. Turn right onto Cards Mill Road. In 1 mile, turn left onto Baker Hill Road (which becomes Kingsley Road in Lebanon). In 0.6 mile, the Air Line State Park Trail crosses the road; park along the right side of the road.

To reach the southernmost parking location in East Hampton, take CT 2 to Exit 13 and follow CT 66 south 4 miles. Turn left onto CT 196/Lakeview St. and drive 0.5 mile, then turn left onto Flanders Road and drive 0.25 mile. Turn right onto Smith St.; the trailhead is on the left.

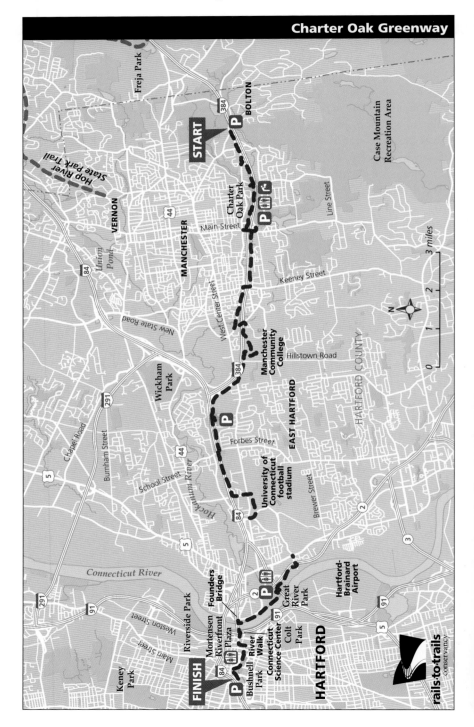

Charter Oak Greenway

The paved Charter Oak Greenway rolls more than 13 miles through the tree-covered hills and eastern suburbs of Hartford before crossing the Connecticut River and ending in the capital's downtown. At first glance, the trail looks as if it is simply a highway side path, but the journey from east to west takes trail users through a variety of experiences, including college campuses, community parks, forests, commercial areas, a peaceful riverfront, and a vibrant city center.

Beginning at the eastern trailhead at Porter Street and Camp Meeting Road in Manchester, you will find ample parking, well-maintained gardens, and an information kiosk. Development on an extension heading east from this trailhead is already in progress. Near its east end

The path offers some fun twists and turns as it winds up a hill in Manchester.

County
Hartford

Endpoints
Porter St. and Camp Meeting Road/CT 534 (Manchester) to Forbes St., just north of Ridgewood Road (East Hartford), and Willow St. and Main St. (East Hartford) to Bushnell Park (15 Trinity St.) (Hartford)

Mileage
13.4

Type
Greenway/Non-Rail-Trail

Roughness Index
1

Surface
Asphalt

Charter Oak Park, on the eastern leg of the trail, provides access to restrooms, drinking water, and other amenities.

is the Hop River State Park Trail (see page 26), which spans 20 miles largely through dense woodlands. Less than 2 miles separate the two trails, and plans are in the works to connect them. Both are part of the expansive East Coast Greenway, which will one day connect multiuse trails from Maine to Florida.

From the eastern trailhead of the Charter Oak Greenway, the well-signed and newly paved trail parallels Highland Street before descending into the Birch Mountain Brook stream valley. Here along a tree-lined path, with the bubbling brook flowing beside you, you may forget that I-384 is just over the ridge.

Less than 2 miles from the Porter Street trailhead, you arrive at Charter Oak Park, a lovely community park in Manchester providing access to restrooms, water, ball fields, tennis courts, a pavilion, and gardens. This intersection with the town provides an opportunity to find trailside amenities and a bite to eat. Proceeding west from Charter Oak Park, the trail passes through handsomely appointed residential and commercial communities. You'll need to navigate a 0.5-mile on-road portion of trail along Hartford Road and Bidwell Street before leaving the road to enter the campus of Manchester Community College.

Now off road once again, the trail traverses the college campus through sports fields and pine forest before leaving campus to head toward Hartford. Although I-384 is nearby, the trail shares the right-of-way with a utility corridor, and the emergence of tall grasses within it provides a meadowlike atmosphere as the trail approaches downtown. Prior to reaching Hartford, the path takes you past the University of Connecticut football stadium in East Hartford. The route will travel on-road again for the approximately 1-mile gap to the Hockanum

River. The trail becomes off-road again at the intersection of Willow Street and Main Street in East Hartford.

As the path approaches the east bank of the Connecticut River, it has a decidedly more parklike feel. As you continue, the Connecticut River will be on your left and mature trees abound. Park users may be seen all around you, enjoying the amenities, sights, and sounds of Great River Park, with its expansive views of the Hartford skyline across the river.

Heading north along the river, trail users may appreciate the many sculptures and other artwork located along the riverfront before the route ascends a flood-control levy to reach Founders Bridge. The trail crosses the Connecticut River and arrives in downtown Hartford.

Once downtown, continue on the River Walk, a series of raised plazas and pedestrian areas hovering two stories above the city streets. On these busy plazas and public gathering spaces, cyclists are advised to walk their bikes, but it's a good place to slow down and savor the views; look up at the skyscrapers surrounding you, or glimpse down at the Connecticut River. Trail users remain elevated for several blocks from the Mortensen Riverfront Plaza to Prospect Street. Be sure to peruse the prominently displayed art and nearby attractions, such as the Connecticut Science Center.

From Prospect Street to Bushnell Park, the trail meanders a half dozen well-marked blocks before terminating in the expansive urban oasis of Bushnell Park near the impressive State Capitol Building, ending your journey from verdant rolling hills to vibrant urban center.

CONTACT: ct.gov/dot

DIRECTIONS

To reach the parking lot of the eastern trailhead from Hartford, take I-384 to Exit 4. Turn left onto Wyllys St., then take an immediate right onto Highland St./CT 534. Proceed on Highland St. 0.3 mile; the parking lot will be on your left. From the east, take Exit 4 off of I-384 and turn right directly onto Highland St. The trailhead will be on your left in 0.6 mile.

To reach the western trailhead in Bushnell Park (15 Trinity St., Hartford), take I-91 to Exit 29A and continue on Whitehead Hwy. In 0.2 mile, at the traffic circle (Pulaski Cir.), take the second exit (straight) to Elm St. and continue 0.3 mile to Trinity St. Turn right to reach Bushnell Park.

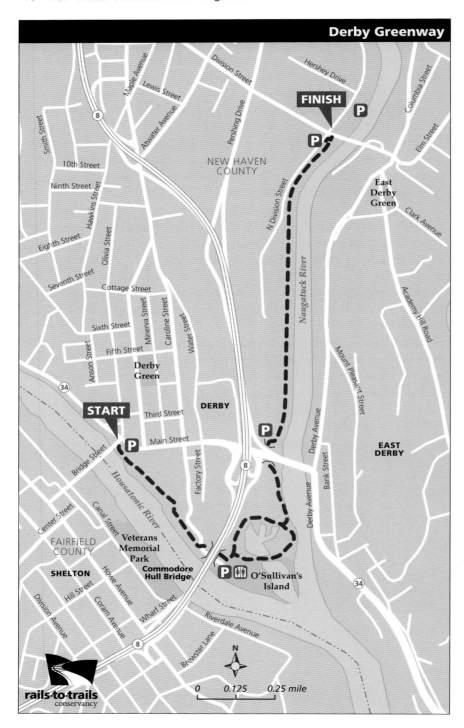

Derby Greenway

FINISH

NEW HAVEN
COUNTY

East
Derby
Green

START

Derby
Green

DERBY

EAST
DERBY

O'Sullivan's
Island

FAIRFIELD
COUNTY

SHELTON

Veterans
Memorial
Park

Commodore
Hull Bridge

Maple Avenue
Lewis Street
Atwater Avenue
Division Street
Hershey Drive
Columbia Street
Elm Street
Smith Street
10th Street
Ninth Street
Hawkins Street
Pershing Drive
N Division Street
Clark Avenue
Eighth Street
Olivia Street
Naugatuck River
Academy Hill Road
Seventh Street
Cottage Street
Sixth Street
Minerva Street
Caroline Street
Water Street
Fifth Street
Anson Street
Mount Pleasant Street
Third Street
Derby Avenue
Bank Street
Main Street
Bridge Street
Factory Street
Housatonic River
Center Street
Canal Street
Howe Avenue
Coram Avenue
Wharf Street
Riverdale Avenue
Division Avenue
Hill Street
Brewster Lane

N

0   0.125   0.25 mile

rails·to·trails
conservancy

Running alongside both the Housatonic and Naugatuck Rivers, the Derby Greenway demonstrates a seamless integration of Connecticut's natural river systems and parks with man-made interventions of the past and present. The new addition of a striking sea green bike-pedestrian bridge on the southern end of the trail exemplifies Derby's ambition to reinvent itself as a modern town while simultaneously providing views of a historical rail line bridge and flood-control dikes that speak to the city's history.

Derby's success as a city is largely attributed to its ability to continually evolve its use of the Naugatuck and Housatonic Rivers over time. The rivers initially supported fishing and transportation industries, eventually became a seaport and site for shipbuilding, and at their prime served as the backbone for the town's industrial sector. Eventually, Derby would become another example of

Running alongside both the Housatonic and Naugatuck Rivers, the Derby Greenway offers scenic views the whole way.

County
New Haven

Endpoints
Bridge St. and Main St. to Division St. and N. Division St. (Derby)

Mileage
2.0

Type
Greenway/Rail-with-Trail

Roughness Index
1

Surfaces
Asphalt, Dirt

post-industrial decline in America, but as the city strives to recruit residents, the rivers have served as a critical asset to the future of this small Connecticut town.

At the beginning of the trail, by the Main Street parking lot, guests are introduced to the transformative value of the Housatonic and Naugatuck Rivers. Beyond their aesthetic and recreational values, they have also played a role in the restoration of the historical Birmingham National Bank, built in 1893, into a restaurant and weekend live entertainment venue, creating greater activity around the Derby Greenway.

Across from the National Bank, trail visitors begin their route on a 10-foot-wide path atop the dike containing the Housatonic River, which was erected after the great 1955 floods that devastated communities near the Housatonic and Naugatuck Rivers. The path leads to a new bike-pedestrian bridge that provides trail users with a great view of the Housatonic River. The trail exits the dike and descends to the boat launch area under the Commodore Hull Bridge, where parking and restroom facilities are provided.

The trail then meanders across O'Sullivan's Island, actually a peninsula, where visitors travel on a dirt path within open park space that hosts myriad deciduous trees, many towering over the park. The trail passes through the peninsula and is flanked by a small swampy area to the east with expansive views of the Housatonic to the west. Leaving the peninsula, the route passes under CT 34 alongside a wooden barricade that separates trail users from an active rail line that runs on top of the Naugatuck River dike. The paved trail continues along the river, providing views of wildlife such as geese and hawks diving into the water for fish.

The path ends at Division Street, where a small rest space with brick flooring, a couple of benches, and a fountain dedicated by the National Humane Alliance beautify the connection between a parking lot and the trail. Across from the parking lot is a shopping center and supermarket.

CONTACT: derbyct.gov/Derby-Greenway and naugatuckriver.net/index.php /greenway/about-the-greenway

DIRECTIONS

From I-84, take Exit 19 to merge onto CT 8 S. In 17.8 miles, take Exit 15 for CT 34 toward Derby/ New Haven. Turn onto CT 34/Main St. going westbound for 0.3 mile and then turn left onto Bridge St.; the parking lot will be on your left immediately after turning.

First a canal, then a railroad, and now a trail define the history of the Farmington Canal Heritage Trail. Completed segments span Connecticut south to north, from New Haven to the Massachusetts border, for nearly 50 miles. A multiyear work in progress with only a couple of gaps remaining, the trail will total 57 miles when finished. Across the state border, the trail connects with Southwick Rail Trail (see page 99), part of a developing trail system that will one day span 25 miles to Northampton, creating a key interstate route.

The paved pathway follows the Farmington Canal, once the longest in New England. Built between 1824 and 1835 to get farm products to market on boats towed by horses and mules, it became obsolete in the railroad age. The New Haven and Northampton Company replaced the canal with a railroad between New Haven and Plainville by 1847. Mergers and acquisitions created the New York, New Haven and Hartford Railroad, which operated until

Counties
Hartford, New Haven

Endpoints
Temple St. between Trumbull St. and Grove St. (New Haven) to Lazy Lane west of Queen St. (Southington) and Northwest Dr. and Johnson Ave. (Plainville) to the CT–MA state line 0.3 mile north of the intersection of Phelps Road and Quarry Road (West Suffield)

Mileage
47.6

Type
Rail-Trail

Roughness Index
1

Surface
Asphalt

The northern section of the trail offers a journey through hardwood forests.

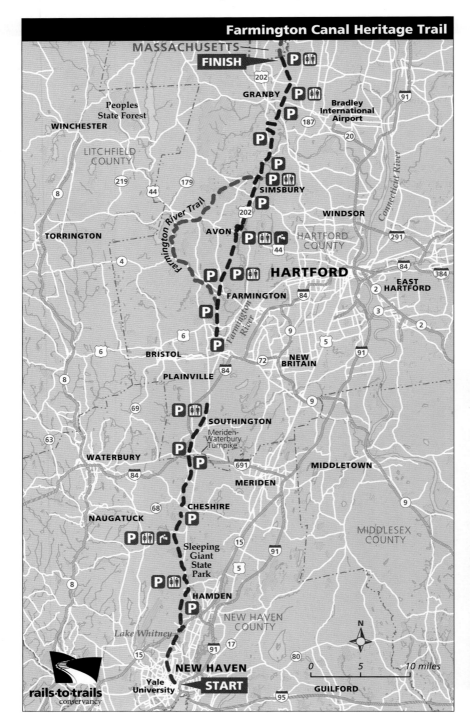

Farmington Canal Heritage Trail

1969 when it was consolidated into Penn Central. As the rail corridor became disused in the 1980s, a citizens group pushed for the rail-trail project. The first section opened in 1993.

Today, the trail runs through the population centers around New Haven in the south to the more rural communities, forests, and farms in the north. From Simsbury south to New Haven, the trail is part of the East Coast Greenway, a developing trail network that will span the Atlantic Seaboard. It also meets both ends of the 16.5-mile Farmington River Trail (see page 23), which is shaped like a C between Simsbury and Farmington.

Southern Section: New Haven to Southington

Yale University anchors the trail's southern terminus, with easiest access off Hill-house Avenue. (Plans are under way to extend the trail another 2 miles to Long Wharf Nature Preserve in New Haven Harbor.) Heading north, the path travels through a narrow park. As you enter Hamden in 2.5 miles, you'll pass through nearly 3 miles of green space surrounding Lake Whitney, which provides a reserve source of drinking water to the area.

Entering the Mount Carmel neighborhood, on the right you'll pass Sleeping Giant State Park, which rises to a rocky outcrop and summit observation tower. With a little imagination, the mountain appears as a reclining giant from head to toe.

You can learn more about the historical canal at the Lock 12 Historical Park in Cheshire. After a 0.7-mile detour on Willow Street between Cornwall Avenue and Mill Street (slated for a connection with an elevated boardwalk through a swamp by 2019), you'll get another history lesson at the circa 1890 Southington Train Depot and Museum just past Meriden-Waterbury Turnpike/CT 322 in Southington.

Northern Section: Plainville to the Connecticut-Massachusetts State Line

The longest gap on the trail is between Lazy Lane in Southington and Northwest Drive in Plainville. The railroad corridor is still in use through this area, but an off-road trail option is being studied. Trail parking is available on either side of this gap at Mill Street in Southington and Northwest Drive in Plainville.

Arriving at Red Oak Hill Road in Farmington, you can go straight to stay on the canal trail or left to the trailhead of the Farmington River Trail. Both end up in Simsbury, though the river trail is 16.5 miles compared to 11 miles on the canal trail. Bump-outs on the 400-foot former railroad bridge across the Farmington River allow trail users a better view of the river.

Not far up the trail you'll enter hardwood forests around Avon. The route takes a 1.8-mile detour on sidewalks and paths around the town center. Follow the bike route signs to the trailhead in Sperry Park. The trail rolls through suburban neighborhoods and past light industrial parks for 4.2 miles to Simsbury, where you'll hit the connection to the Farmington River Trail at Drake Hill Road and Hopmeadow Street. A half mile ahead on the left you'll see the Simsbury Railroad Depot, built in 1875; it's a restaurant now.

The trail heads north from the depot 10.3 miles through farms and forests to the state line. Along the way, you'll pass pockets of residential and commercial development.

CONTACT: farmingtoncanal.org and fchtrail.org

DIRECTIONS

To reach the trailhead on the Yale University campus from I-91, take Exit 3 and merge onto Trumbull St. Go 0.3 mile and turn left onto Hillhouse Ave. The trailhead is on the right. Look for on-street or garage parking; campus parking is free on weekends and after 4:30 p.m. on weekdays.

To reach the trailhead on Mill St. in Southington from I-84 N, take Exit 30 and turn left onto Atwater St. toward Southington. Go 400 feet and turn right onto Marion Ave., and then go another 400 feet and turn left onto West St. In 1.1 miles turn right onto Mill St., and then go 0.9 mile to parking on the left. From I-84 S, take Exit 30 and turn left onto Marion Ave. Go 0.2 mile and turn left onto West St. Go 1.1 miles and turn onto Mill St., and then go 0.9 mile to parking on the left.

To reach the trail near Northwest Dr. in Plainville from I-84 E, take Exit 37 and turn left onto Fienemann Road toward Farmington. Go 0.5 mile and turn left onto US 6/Colt Hwy. Go 2.5 miles and turn left onto CT 552/Scott Swamp Road, and then go 0.2 mile and turn right onto CT 10/Main St. In 0.9 mile turn right onto Northwest Dr. Go 0.8 mile and look for parking on the right. From I-84 W, take Exit 39 and merge onto US 6 W. In 3.2 miles turn left onto CT 552/Scott Swamp Road, and follow the directions above from there.

To reach the trail near Red Oak Hill Road in Farmington from I-84 E, take Exit 37 and turn left onto Fienemann Road toward Farmington. Go 0.5 mile and turn left onto US 6/Colt Hwy. Go 1.3 miles and turn right onto Reservoir Road, and then go 0.4 mile and turn left onto Diamond Glen Road/Hatter Lane. Go 0.6 mile and turn left onto CT 10/Main St., and in one block turn right onto Meadow Road, which becomes Red Oak Hill Road. Go 1.3 miles and turn right onto Tunxis Mead Road and look for parking at the athletic fields. To reach the trail, return to Red Oak Hill Road, turn right, and follow the sidewalk 0.3 mile to the trailhead. From I-84 W, take Exit 38 and merge onto US 6. In 2.1 miles turn right onto Reservoir Road and follow the directions above from there.

To reach the northern trailhead from I-91, take Exit 40 onto CT 20/Bradley International Airport Connector. Go 6.2 miles on CT 20, and turn right onto Newgate Road. Go 1.8 miles and turn left onto Copper Hill Road, and then go 0.2 mile and turn right onto Griffin Road/Copper Hill Road. Go 1.9 miles and turn left onto Phelps Road. Travel 0.7 mile and look for parking on the left.

A dozen miles west of Connecticut's capital of Hartford, the Farmington River Trail forms a 16.5-mile arc that connects to the larger Farmington Canal Heritage Trail (see page 19) on both ends. The rail-trail was built largely on the former Central New England Railway right-of-way.

Beginning in Farmington, you'll follow the river northwest through residential areas and past old trees. There are many points along this trail where you can stop and savor breathtaking views of the Farmington River, which is a National Wild and Scenic River, and perhaps even spot a heron resting on a rock. Winding through tree canopies and past old mills, rapids, and waterfalls, this paved portion of the trail connects Unionville, Collinsville, and Canton. The off-road trail experience ends in the lovely town of Canton, 10 miles from the start of your trip.

Winding through woodlands alongside the Farmington River, the trail provides a pleasant ride.

County
Hartford

Endpoints
Red Oak Hill Road at New Britain Ave. (Farmington) to Riverside Road near Drake Hill Road (Simsbury)

Mileage
16.5

Type
Rail-Trail

Roughness Index
1

Surfaces
Asphalt, Crushed Stone

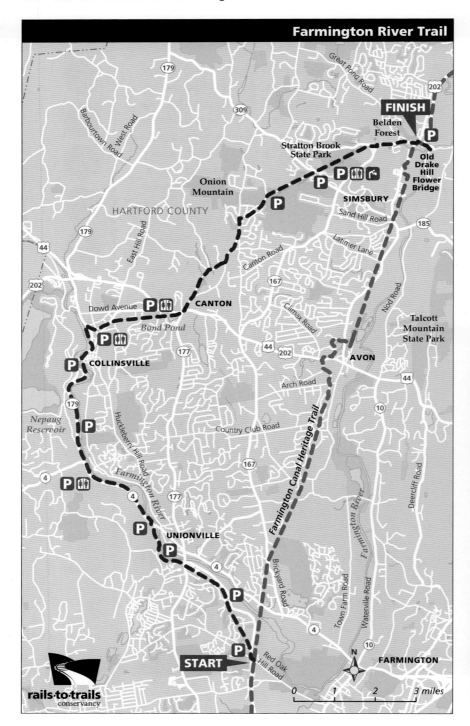

Farmington River Trail

179

Great Pond Road

202

309

FINISH

Belden
Forest

P

Barbourtown Road

West Road

Stratton Brook
State Park

P P 🚻 ⛱

Old
Drake
Hill
Flower
Bridge

Onion
Mountain

P

SIMSBURY

Sand Hill Road

185

HARTFORD COUNTY

East Hill Road

179

Latimer Lane

44

Canton Road

Climax Road

202

167

Talcott
Mountain
State Park

Dowd Avenue P 🚻   **CANTON**

Bond Pond

P 🚻

177

44 202

AVON

44

P **COLLINSVILLE**

Arch Road

10

179

Farmington Canal Heritage Trail

*Nepaug
Reservoir*

P

Huckleberry Hill Road

Country Club Road

167

Deercliff Road

4

P 🚻

Farmington River

4 177

P

UNIONVILLE

P

4

Brickyard Road

Town Farm Road

Waterville Road

10

P

N

FARMINGTON

START ▶ P

Red Oak
Hill Road

4

0   1   2   3 miles

rails·to·trails
conservancy

North of Canton, the route transitions to on-road sharrows (markings that indicate a shared bicycle-vehicle lane). Follow the bike route signs on these lightly trafficked roads to Simsbury. At the intersection of Town Forest Road and Stratton Brook Road, a small section of the Farmington River Trail is once again off-road. This portion of the trail has a stone-dust surface and traverses Stratton Brook State Park. The densely wooded park offers hiking, swimming, and fishing opportunities.

When you reach Bushy Hill Road, note that you'll have to turn left and cross West Street to pick up another section of paved trail, which parallels the north side of West Street. When you arrive at Drake Hill Road, you'll cross West Street again and parallel Drake Hill Road toward the Farmington River. Crossing the river on Old Drake Hill Flower Bridge provides a charming end to your journey. The metal-truss bridge was built in 1892 and is listed on the National Register of Historic Places. True to its name, it includes 62 flower boxes.

If you're up for more riding, another connection to the Farmington Canal Heritage Trail can be made just before the Flower Bridge at Hopmeadow Street/ US 202, forming a loop between the two trails.

CONTACT: fchtrail.org

DIRECTIONS

To reach the southern end, take I-84 to Exit 39 and follow CT 508 east for 1.5 miles (it becomes CT 4). Turn left onto CT 10 S, and in 1 mile, turn right onto Meadow Road. Follow this road 1.6 miles (it becomes Red Oak Hill Road), then take a right onto New Britain Ave. and the parking lot will be on your left.

To reach the northern end, if you're coming from Hartford, take US 44 W 9 miles to a right turn on US 202 E in Avon. Take US 202 N 4.7 miles to a right turn on Drake Hill Road. Travel 0.1 mile to a left turn on Iron Horse Blvd. Take your next left into the parking area.

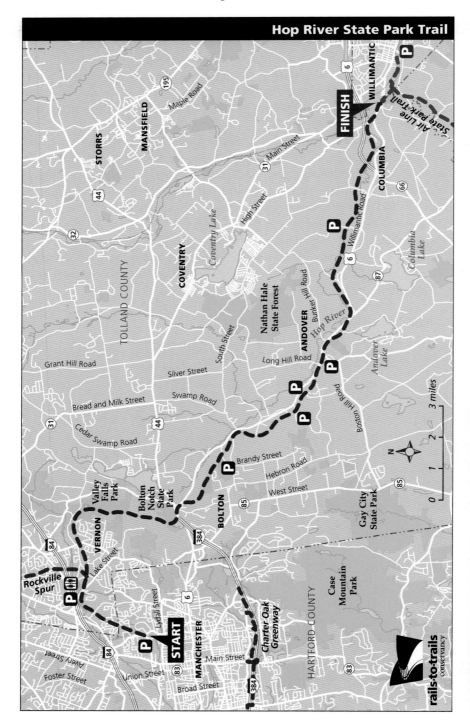

Hop River State Park Trail

It's hard to pick a favorite season to experience the Hop River State Park Trail, set amid the dense forests of Eastern Connecticut. Sections of the 20-mile rail-trail dive through steep rock cuts that seep moisture, supplying air-conditioning in summer and freezing into glistening icefalls in winter. Maples and oaks bring fiery autumn hues, and in the spring, trilliums and other wildflowers speckle the ground with color. Three tunnels and a covered bridge complete the trail's picturesque backdrop.

Following the former Hartford, Providence and Fishkill Railroad, the rail-trail feels like it's transporting visitors to the days when rail was the predominant mode of transportation. The telegraph poles from days gone by still jut out of the hillside, and a few miles into the trail from the western side, you can see a turnabout that was used to reverse the direction of the train.

The picturesque rail-trail dives through steep rock cuts and dense forests.

Counties
Hartford, Tolland

Endpoints
Colonial Road and Parker St. (Manchester) to Columbia Ave./ CT 66 at the Willimantic River bridge, 0.1 mile east of Cards Mill Road (Willimantic)

Mileage
20.0

Type
Rail-Trail

Roughness Index
1–2

Surface
Crushed Stone

After beginning your ride in Manchester, you'll have the opportunity to connect to another trail in 2.6 miles. At Church and Phoenix Streets in Vernon, a trail called the Rockville Spur (sometimes known as Vernon Rails-to-Trails) branches north. If you have time, the scenic 4.2-mile pathway (see page 54) is definitely worth exploring.

From that trail intersection continuing east on the Hop River State Park Trail, you'll climb gradually for a few miles past rock outcrops. Along the way, you'll pass Valley Falls Park, then Bolton Notch State Park, both of which are accessible via hiking paths that spin off from the rail-trail.

Beyond the Bolton Notch parking lot, the trail passes beneath US 44 and US 6, threading through a narrow rock cut and then descending several miles among thick woodlands. Past Steeles Crossing Road in Bolton, US 6 comes into view on your left, but not so close as to disrupt the tranquil experience. Keep watch for small waterfalls like the one near Burnap Brook Road, and enjoy the covered bridge over CT 316.

In another mile, you pass beneath US 6 through a 100-foot lighted tunnel. The route continues along the river to its end at Columbia Avenue in Willimantic. Here, a bridge over the Willimantic River connects the trail to the Air Line State Park Trail (see page 8), which spans more than 50 miles, running northeast to the Massachusetts border and southwest to East Hampton.

CONTACT: **www.ct.gov/deep/hoprivertrail**

DIRECTIONS

Below we've listed two parking waypoints for the trail, but there are several other parking options as well; for more information on those, use the link above or **TrailLink.com.**

To reach the west end of the trail in Manchester, from I-84, take Exit 63 for CT 30/Windsor. Head southeast (left if you took I-84 E and right if you took I-84 W) on CT 30 N. In 0.2 mile (0.4 mile if you took I-84 W), turn right onto Parker St. Follow Parker 0.9 mile, then turn left onto Colonial Road. Look for the trailhead parking lot immediately to your left.

To reach the eastern trailhead parking lot in Columbia (which lies 3.5 miles from the trail's end), take I-384 to US 6, and continue east on US 6 for 9.3 miles. Turn left onto Hop River Road. The parking lot will appear on your left in 0.4 mile.

The 3.1-mile Kress Family Trail in Roxbury occupies the former route of the Shepaug Valley Railroad (the Shepaug, Litchfield and Northern Railroad). The railroad was famously known as the "crookedest railroad east of California," meandering 32 miles to cover a distance of 18 miles as the crow flies. The trail charts a serpentine course through the river valley, linking the Orzech Family Preserve to the River Road, Erbacher, and Golden Harvest Preserves. The Roxbury Land Trust manages these natural areas.

The best place to start is the entrance to the Orzech Family Preserve on Botsford Hill Road, near the sky-blue barns of Orzech Farm. There is parking here, as well as a kiosk with a map and tips for encountering wildlife (bears, specifically). Past the gate, you will find yourself plunged into a fairy-tale forest, where rows of slender hemlock

The rustic path traverses the lushly wooded Shepaug River valley.

County
Litchfield

Endpoints
Botsford Hill Road near Baker Road/CT 67 to Minor Bridge Road west of Falls Road (Roxbury)

Mileage
3.1

Type
Rail-Trail

Roughness Index
2

Surface
Dirt

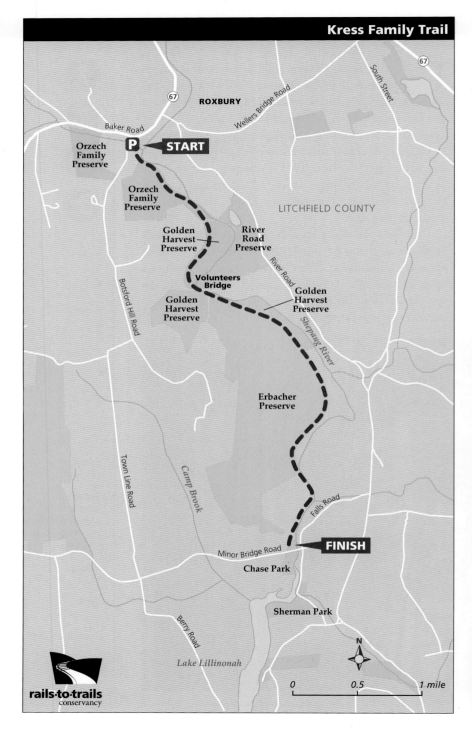

Kress Family Trail

(67)

South Street

ROXBURY

Wellers Bridge Road

Baker Road

Orzech
Family
Preserve

P ◀ **START**

Orzech
Family
Preserve

LITCHFIELD COUNTY

Golden
Harvest
Preserve

River
Road
Preserve

River Road

**Volunteers
Bridge**

Golden
Harvest
Preserve

Golden
Harvest
Preserve

Botsford Hill Road

Shepaug River

Erbacher
Preserve

Town Line Road

Camp Brook

Falls Road

Minor Bridge Road

FINISH ◀

Chase Park

Sherman Park

Berry Road

N

Lake Lillinonah

0   0.5   1 mile

rails·to·trails
conservancy

trees envelop the trail in a leafy embrace. Offshoot hiking paths peel off from the rail-trail, taking travelers deeper into the woods. Blue blazes mark trees along these paths for navigation.

Although you can catch glimpses of the Shepaug River between the trees, Volunteers Bridge offers the best viewpoint of the watercourse. This quirky wooden footbridge was built by—as you may have guessed—volunteers from Roxbury, and clearly takes its inspiration from truss railroad bridges of years past. It's located 1.4 miles from the trailhead. Across the bridge is the River Road Preserve, with picnic tables, a map kiosk, and more trails. Back on the trail, the route winds through verdant woodland and bucolic meadows to finally end on Minor Bridge Road. Hikers may decide to lengthen their excursion by retracing their steps and ending their journey at the main trailhead on Botsford Hill Road.

Though the trail is open for cycling, its uneven surface makes for a bumpy ride in places. You are welcome to bring your dog, but dogs must remain leashed.

CONTACT: roxburylandtrust.org/preserves.html

DIRECTIONS

To reach the Orzech Family Preserve entrance from I-84, take Exit 9 for CT 25 toward Brookfield. Head north on Hawleyville Road/CT 25, and go 3.5 miles. Turn right onto CT 133 and continue on it 6.3 miles, then take a right onto Clapboard Road. In 1.2 miles, make a right turn onto CT 67, and in 1 mile make a final right turn onto Botsford Hill Road. The preserve entrance will be on your right.

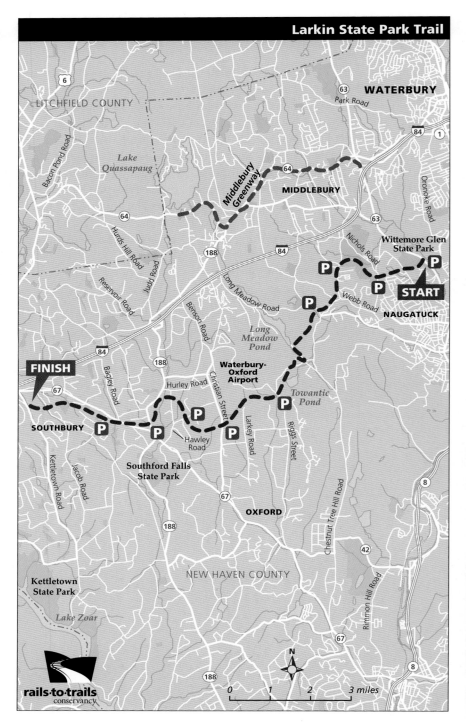

Larkin State Park Trail

The Larkin State Park Trail meanders 10.8 miles through the woods and around the lakes and low hills of southwestern Connecticut. The rail-trail follows the route of the New York & New England Railroad, founded in 1873 (with this section built in 1881) and succeeded by the New York, New Haven and Hartford Railroad in 1898.

The trail's former name—the Larkin State Bridle Trail—attests to its origins as an equestrian trail. A local surgeon, Dr. Charles Larkin, bought the disused railbed and donated it to the state in 1943. Horseback riders use this trail frequently and have the right-of-way. Bicyclists should remember to approach horses slowly and quietly, speaking softly and taking cues from their riders. If necessary, dismount on the low side of the trail, as horses instinctively fear anything that might pounce from above.

While railroad builders avoided steep hillsides with a serpentine route and railroad cuts, the trail slopes gently

The trail meanders through the tranquil woodlands of southwestern Connecticut.

County
New Haven

Endpoints
Straits Turnpike/Church St./CT 63 between Allerton Farms Road and Mill St. (Naugatuck) to Kettletown Road between Southford Road/CT 67 and Elk Dr. (Southbury)

Mileage
10.8

Type
Rail-Trail

Roughness Index
2–3

Surfaces
Cinder, Crushed Stone, Dirt, Gravel

uphill from each end to the high point at Prokop Road/Riggs Street in Oxford. The path also ascends or descends steeply at some road crossings. While the trail's surface is typically firm, sections in the west can be rough or soggy, making mountain bikes or hybrid bikes with wide tires a preferred choice.

Even though the trail rolls through the outskirts of the Colonial-era towns of Naugatuck, Middlebury, Oxford, and Southbury, there are no services along the trail, so stock up with food and water.

Starting at the parking lot on CT 63 in Naugatuck, you'll pass through heavily wooded Whittemore Glen State Park. Forests border the route most of the way to the trail's end in Southbury, making this an ideal destination for leaf-peeping in autumn.

After nearly 4 miles, the trail passes the southern tip of Long Meadow Pond, inaccessible behind private properties. At Long Meadow Road, you'll briefly leave state-owned property for a 0.5-mile on-road detour around a privately held stretch. Turn left onto Long Meadow Road and right onto Towantic Hill Road, then watch for trail access on the left side of the road.

Back on the pathway, you'll get views of Towantic Pond's boggy shoreline and pass over wetlands on a causeway. The trail brushes the southern end of the Waterbury-Oxford Airport at 5.7 miles, and then passes through more woods on its final run to Kettletown Road in Southbury.

CONTACT: www.ct.gov/deep/larkin

DIRECTIONS

To reach the eastern trailhead in Naugatuck from I-84 W/Yankee Expwy. southeast of Waterbury, take Exit 17 onto CT 64/Chase Pkwy. Go 0.3 mile and turn left onto CT 63/Straits Turnpike. Go 2.5 miles and look for parking on the right at the sign for LARKIN STATE BRIDLE TRAIL. From I-84 E, take Exit 17, and turn right onto CT 63/Straits Turnpike. Go 2 miles and look for parking on the right at the sign for LARKIN STATE BRIDLE TRAIL.

To reach the western trailhead in Southbury from I-84/Yankee Expwy. east of Waterbury, take Exit 16 and turn left onto CT 188 S/Strongtown Road. Go 2.5 miles and look for parking on the left. The trail ends 2.4 miles west on Kettletown Road.

The Middlebury Greenway provides a paved, off-road option for a self-propelled journey across suburban Middlebury. The trail touches on several business districts and parks, ending at an amusement park dating back more than 100 years, where visitors can still take thrilling rides or go swimming in the lake. Stone benches are placed along the trail for those who occasionally need to take a load off their feet.

The greenway follows the route of an electric trolley line that ran between Waterbury and Woodbury (Middlebury is in between) beginning in 1908. The Connecticut Company trolley not only served commuters but also

Short but sweet, the greenway offers many lovely sights across its 4.5 miles.

County
New Haven

Endpoints
Straits Turnpike/CT 63 at Woodside Ave. to Middlebury Road/CT 64 between Old Woodbury Road and Christian Road (Middlebury)

Mileage
4.5

Type
Rail-Trail

Roughness Index
1

Surface
Asphalt

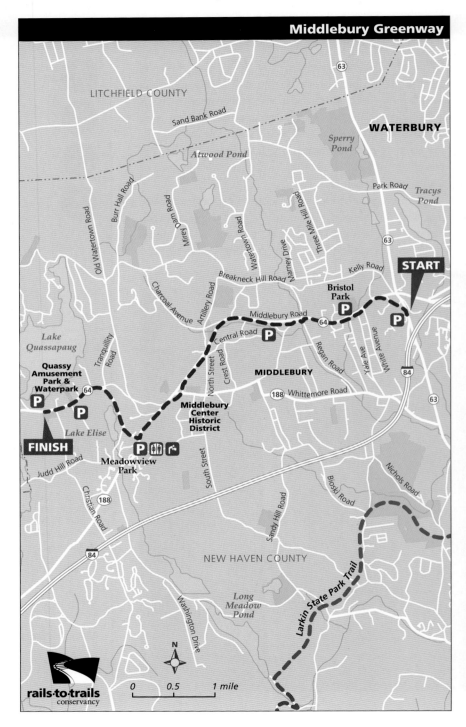

Middlebury Greenway

LITCHFIELD COUNTY

63

Sand Bank Road

Atwood Pond

WATERBURY

Sperry
Pond

Park Road

Tracys
Pond

Burr Hall Road

Old Watertown Road

Mitten Dam Road

Watertown Road

Three Mile Hill Road

Narney Drive

63

Park Road

Breakneck Hill Road

Kelly Road

START

Charcoal Avenue

Artillery Road

Middlebury Road

64

Bristol
Park

P

P

Lake
Quassapaug

Tranquillity Road

Central Road

P

North Street

Crest Road

MIDDLEBURY

Regan Road

Yale Ave

White Avenue

84

63

Quassy
Amusement
Park &
Waterpark

64

P

P

Middlebury
Center
Historic
District

188

Whittemore Road

Lake Elise

FINISH

P 👥 🚻

Judd Hill Road

Meadowview
Park

South Street

Bioski Road

Nichols Road

Christian Road

188

84

Sandy Hill Road

NEW HAVEN COUNTY

Larkin State Park Trail

Long
Meadow
Pond

N

Washington Drive

rails·to·trails
conservancy

0   0.5   1 mile

The serpentine route includes several brook crossings.

delivered tourists to a resort it built and owned on a 300-acre Middlebury lake. The so-called trolley park was named Lake Quassapaug Amusement Park, but guests shortened it to Quassy and the name stuck. After the state upgraded CT 64 as a parallel road to the trolley line, people opted to drive out to the lake instead. The trolley shut down in 1930, but the park opens every summer.

The Middlebury Greenway has a slight uphill slope if you begin at the eastern trailhead on CT 63, so you'll finish heading downhill if you're making an out-and-back trek. In 0.3 mile, you'll parallel CT 64/Middlebury Road, which will be your companion for the rest of the trip. The trail remains on the south side of the road. You'll also frequently cross numerous side streets that feed into CT 64, especially in the first couple of miles, so always be aware of the crossings.

Almost immediately you'll see heavily wooded Bristol Park across CT 64 from the Middlebury Greenway. Several trails and a stream go through the park. Although many homes line the path, you'll pass by several roadside business districts. You're never far from cafés, taverns, or small food stores.

At 1.1 miles, you'll pass the Vaszauskas Farm stand, where you can purchase fresh fruits and vegetables, as well as plants and flowers. In another 1.7 miles, you'll pass underneath Whittemore Road/West Street. If you turn left here, heading off the trail and traveling on-road for 0.2 mile along Whittemore Road, you'll enter the Middlebury Center Historic District, which is replete with white multistory homes and church steeples surrounding a village green. The

Westover School, a girls' college-prep boarding school, has sat on the corner of Whittemore Road and South Street since 1909.

Back on the trail, you'll pass Meadowview Park in 0.9 mile after the underpass, and the entrance to Quassy Amusement Park & Waterpark in another 0.8 mile. The park transformed from a summer resort to a full-blown amusement park after three businessmen bought it from the parent company of the trolley line in 1937. Over the years they kept adding attractions to the dance hall and beach areas. Today, the park features a roller coaster, kiddie rides, a water park, and more. Admission is free if you want to just look around or load up on fried dough and ice cream.

CONTACT: ct.gov/dot

DIRECTIONS

To reach the eastern trailhead from I-84 E, take Exit 17 and turn left onto Straits Turnpike/ CT 63. Go 0.2 mile and turn left onto Woodside Ave. and immediately turn right into Maggie McFly's restaurant. Parking is available for trail users in the upper lot in back. Return to Woodside Ave. and follow the sidewalk on the left side of the entrance. From I-84 W/Yankee Expwy. southeast of Waterbury, take Exit 17 onto CT 64/Chase Pkwy. Go 0.3 mile and turn left onto Straits Turnpike/CT 63. Go 0.2 mile and turn right onto Woodside Ave. and immediately turn right into Maggie McFly's restaurant. Parking is available in the upper parking lot in back. Return to Woodside Ave. and follow the sidewalk on the left side of the entrance.

To reach the western trailhead from I-84, take Exit 16 onto CT 188 N/Strongtown Road. Turn right and go 2.5 miles, and then turn left onto Middlebury Road/CT 64. Go 1.2 miles and turn left into Quassapaug Field and look for parking.

The Pequonnock River Trail is not a name you will see on the ground along this developing trail in southwestern Connecticut. Formalized in 2001 by the state, the regional trail pieced together existing paths that had developed separately on the former Housatonic Railroad line—one of New England's first—from urban Bridgeport to rural Monroe, with additional segments opening since then. Indeed, the names you will see along the route or in other sources—such as Housatonic Railway Rails to Trails or Monroe Housatonic Railbed Trail—reflect this railroad heritage.

The first of a handful of disconnected trail segments begins at the Bridgeport Transportation Center in downtown Bridgeport and extends north to North Avenue (US 1), immediately paralleling Housatonic Avenue for its entire route. The paved side path was built in 2001 on the site of the piers of the Housatonic Railroad's former

Near the north end of the trail, Wolfe Park provides an overlook of Great Hollow Lake.

County
Fairfield

Endpoints
Bridgeport Transportation Center on Housatonic Ave./Water St. at Gold St. (Bridgeport) to Swamp Road, 0.1 mile south of Botsford Hill Road (Monroe–Newtown town line)

Mileage
13.6

Type
Rail-Trail

Roughness Index
1–2

Surfaces
Asphalt, Crushed Stone

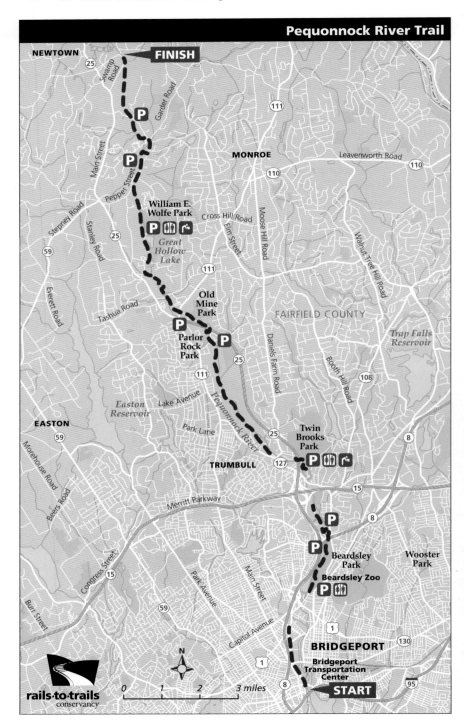

Pequonnock River Trail

Berkshire Spur, an elevated line that once served a handful of industrial customers to the north. Due to its lack of scenery and short length, this portion is often omitted from Pequonnock River Trail itineraries, though it is well used and appreciated by Bridgeport residents reaching bus and train lines by foot.

A short but difficult to traverse gap separates the Berkshire Spur stretch of the Pequonnock River Trail from a newer portion farther north. That stretch—a more popular starting point for recreational trail users—begins at the residential corner of Crown Street and Glenwood Avenue and extends north along the edge of the adjacent Beardsley Zoo, the only zoo in Connecticut, and Beardsley Park. Frederick Law Olmsted designed the park, which offers numerous playing fields among its rolling acres.

North of the park, the trail passes under CT 8 and Old Town Road and crosses the Pequonnock River. From here, the path runs immediately adjacent to Quarry Road past commercial buildings to a dead-end south of Merritt Parkway (CT 15). At press time, construction was ongoing for the continuation of the trail north, where it will pass via tunnels under Merritt Parkway's on- and off-ramps, as well as reuse a former railroad bridge still standing over the highway. For now, trail users are blocked from continuing northward by the tangle of highways.

North of Merritt Parkway, the shortest stretch of the Pequonnock River Trail—soon to be linked to the portion mentioned above—connects neighborhoods west of CT 25 with Twin Brooks Park in Trumbull. The scenic park features ponds, fields of wildflowers, and hiking trails on its more than 80 acres.

The next section of the Pequonnock River Trail begins on Tait Road in Trumbull. (Trail users coming from Twin Brooks Park can reach the Tait Road starting point via a short jaunt on Manor Drive, Gregory Place, Laurel Street, Daniels Farm Road, and Church Hill Road/CT 127. Note that traffic can be heavy on the latter two roads.) Following its namesake river for more than 3 miles, the trail offers a shady respite from suburban Trumbull. Rapids and distinctive rock outcrops add interest.

While the southern three stretches of the Pequonnock River Trail are entirely asphalt-surfaced, the Trumbull section begins paved but transitions to smooth stone dust where it passes through the stunningly scenic Pequonnock River Valley. The surface is generally compact enough even for wheelchair use here. However, because CT 25 crosses the original railroad right-of-way, there is a short hill to climb in Parlor Rock Park (a late 19th-century amusement area) to access the wooden bridge under the highway.

Continuing northwest, the trail passes through Old Mine Park, paralleling the park entry road. Use caution when crossing the busy Monroe Turnpike (CT 111), where cars often ignore the flashing trail-crossing beacon. Shortly after, the path climbs, temporarily leaving the former rail corridor to bypass marshland. This segment ends on Maple Drive in Monroe, shortly after the low-stress crossing of Victoria Drive.

To continue on the final—and oldest—trail segment, follow Maple Drive north to Purdy Hill Road. Turn right and go a short distance; the route continues on the left via the entrance to William E. Wolfe Park. Largely forested and thus spectacular during autumn, this segment of the trail runs more than 4 miles through the popular park and beyond to the Newtown border. Visiting trail users gravitate to the park, which centers on Great Hollow Lake's attractive sand beach and swimming area and offers restrooms and picnic tables. Nonmotorized boating is permitted on the 16-acre lake, and a paved pedestrian-only walking path circles its shoreline.

Like the stretches through Trumbull and downtown Bridgeport, this section of the Pequonnock River Trail runs on the former Housatonic Railroad corridor; watch for traces of the rail line throughout your journey. The most notable remnant is a stone-arch bridge included on Connecticut's State Register of Historic Places.

The rail-trail crosses area roads several times and includes a short on-road detour at the stone-arch bridge near this trail segment's midpoint. You'll veer through a residential cul-de-sac then turn left and follow Pepper Street 0.25 mile before rejoining the trail. (Note that generic bike route signage is your only indicator that you'll pick up the trail again after the detour.) At the 4-mile mark, you'll cross Pepper Street for the last time. After another 0.25 mile, you'll reach the trail's official end in the woods on the Newtown town line, where overgrown but still in place railroad tracks serve as a final reminder of the rich railroading history of the trail you just traveled. Cross the tracks to continue on one of two parallel, informal, and narrow footpaths that lead north to Swamp Road in Newtown.

CONTACT: pequonnockrivertrail.org

DIRECTIONS

There are several access points and places to park throughout the length of the Pequonnock River Trail.

While there is no access to the northern end in Monroe, a small parking lot on Pepper St. isn't too far away. From I-95, take Exit 27A to head north on CT 25/CT 8. After 3.3 miles, keep left to stay on CT 25. Travel on CT 25 for 8.8 miles, and then take a slight right onto Brook St. Next, turn right onto Pepper St., and travel 2.2 miles. A small gravel parking lot is located on the north side of the road, adjacent to the trail.

At the trail's southern end in Bridgeport, parking is available at a series of parking garages (payment required) along Housatonic Ave. (Water St.) near the Bridgeport Transportation Center. From I-95, take Exit 27A to head north on CT 25/CT 8. Take the first exit (Exit 2) for Golden Hill St., and continue on that road until it ends at Water St. in 0.3 mile. Turn right. A large parking garage can be found just beyond Fairfield Ave. The trail begins one block north.

Additional parking can be found at Beardsley Zoo (off Noble Ave. in Bridgeport), Twin Brooks Park (Trumbull), and William E. Wolfe Park (Monroe). To reach Wolfe Park from I-95, take Exit 27A to head north on CT 25/CT 8. After 3.3 miles, keep left to stay on CT 25. Travel on CT 25 for 7.3 miles, then turn right onto Maple Dr. At the end of Maple Dr. in 0.4 mile, turn right onto Purdy Hill Road, and then take an immediate left into the park. There is a day-use parking fee.

Quinebaug River Trail

The Quinebaug River Trail exists in two segments in northwest Connecticut. The northern section parallels Park Road and Tracy Road for about 2 miles in an industrial section of Putnam with few trail amenities. After a sizable gap, the southern segment of the trail picks up in the town of Killingly. The southern section makes up in charm and scenery what the northern section lacks.

Starting in the town of Killingly, the southern segment of the Quinebaug River Trail heads south for a picturesque journey on a well-maintained riverside pathway through wooded parks and corridors. Parking is available at the intersection of Water Street and Commerce Avenue in downtown Killingly. From here, the route continues south, but be sure to enjoy the views of Fivemile Pond from the bridge spur to the north before proceeding on the main trail south.

The Danielson footbridge offers a charming crossing in Killingly.

County
Windham

Endpoints
Park Road, 0.4 mile north of John Bennett Road, to Park Road and Attawaugan Crossing Road (Putnam); and Prospect Ave. and Palmer St. to Gloria Ave., 0.2 mile north of Robert Ave. (Killingly)

Mileage
4.8

Type
Greenway/Non-Rail-Trail

Roughness Index
1

Surface
Asphalt

After negotiating a series of shared sidewalks and street crossings for 0.5 mile in Killingly, the more appealing character of the trail begins to show. Once you cross Providence Road/US 6, the true off-road experience begins. Take note of the Quinebaug River in the valley below and be ready for a more peaceful trail experience as you leave behind the traffic sounds of town and head closer to the river. As the path veers away from Wauregan Road/CT 12, you pass through a park with ball fields and restrooms.

Continuing south, you'll experience the sights and sounds of the waterway with the river's close proximity. You'll find excellent opportunities to spot riparian wildlife and be able to access a trailside canoe launch. The lush canopy overhead provides shade and dappled sunlight, while ferns and wildflowers flourish below, enhancing the sense of refuge.

It's clear that this well-used trail is enjoyed as a community asset as demonstrated by the popularity of the trail with local joggers, families out for a stroll, and recreational cyclists looking to get out in nature for the afternoon. Four-legged trail users are welcome too, as Mitchell D. Phaiah Dog Park shares a parking lot and trailhead with the trail near the southern terminus in a residential neighborhood near Quinebaug Lake State Park.

The Quinebaug River Trail offers a rewarding experience for those willing to negotiate the less than inspiring section of on-road riding in Killingly. The most scenic southern portion of the route has very few road crossings and an excellent surface. As the trail leaves town and enters the New England wilderness, take in the ample natural beauty as you journey alongside the river among ferns, mature trees, and wildflower meadows.

CONTACT: ct.gov/dot

DIRECTIONS

Unfortunately, there is no dedicated trail parking for the northern segment of the trail.

To access parking for the southern segment, take I-395 to Exit 37 (or Exit 37B if taking I-395 S) for Providence Road/US 6. Merge onto US 6 W. In 0.6 mile turn right onto Main St./CT 12 and then in 0.3 mile turn left onto Commerce Ave. Parking will be on your left at the intersection of Commerce Ave. and Water St. in downtown Killingly.

When complete, Connecticut's Shoreline Greenway Trail will be a scenic 25-mile route through four quaint New England towns off Long Island Sound. From Lighthouse Point to Hammonasset Beach State Park, the trail will connect parks, schools, town centers, train stations, and hiking trails in East Haven, Branford, Guilford, and Madison. A small section of the route, just shy of a mile in Branford, is built along a former railroad bed.

Along the way, enjoy views of the water, forests, meadows, and marshes. Where possible, the trail will be surfaced with distinctive pink crushed granite from a local quarry in Stony Creek. Benches are currently available on the trail, and interpretive signage on the area's unique history and geology, as well as bird-watching stations, are planned for the future.

County
New Haven

Endpoints
Bradford Preserve (near Elliot St. and Henry St.) to Farm River State Park (Short Beach Road/CT 142 near Stone Pillar Road) (East Haven); Tabor Dr. and Ark Road to Blackstone Ave./CT 146 to Thimble Island Road (Branford); and Webster Point Road and Liberty St. to Hammonasset Beach State Park (Hammonasset Connector/CT 450, 0.1 mile south of Boston Post Road/US 1) (Madison)

Mileage
4.1

Type
Rail-Trail/Rail-with-Trail

Roughness Index
1–2

Surfaces
Crushed Stone, Dirt

The Madison Section of the trail allows travelers to explore Hammonasset Beach State Park.

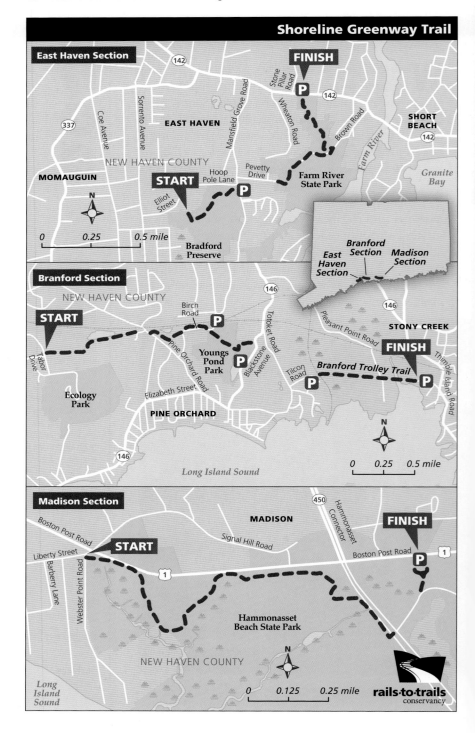

Shoreline Greenway Trail

A boardwalk along the trail provides access to natural areas.

Although many parts of the trail have been cleared for walking and see regular use, sections of the trail are surfaced and fully completed as outlined below from west to east.

East Haven Section

This westernmost section of the Shoreline Greenway Trail, suitable for walking and biking, winds through a heavily wooded area from the former DC Moore Elementary School to the intersection of Hoop Pole Lane and Mansfield Grove Road, a 0.3-mile journey. If entering the trail from Hoop Pole Lane, proceed slowly, as the trail descends a steep dirt hill into the forest.

Travel one block east along Pevetty Drive and the road will dead-end into a pathway that takes trail users into Farm River State Park. Within the park is another 0.6-mile section of the trail that includes two charming footbridges. Unpaved nature trails are also available in the park for further exploring.

Branford Section

A new 0.6-mile section of the trail opened in 2018 and extended the trail westward from Pine Orchard Road to Tabor Drive. From Pine Orchard Road, a 0.9-mile section runs parallel to an active rail line with less than 50 feet of separation at some points, demonstrating the feasibility of such closely located rail and trail facilities. What it lacks in length, it makes up for in scenery; trail goers traverse woodlands and walk or ride past community gardens.

Another 0.6-mile section, known locally as the Branford Trolley Trail, runs from Tilcon Road to Thimble Island Road and stretches between the communities of Pine Orchard and Stony Creek along a former trolley line, offering pleasant views of the Long Island Sound and Thimble Islands.

Madison Section

This easternmost 1.1-mile section leads travelers through Hammonasset Beach State Park with views of woodlands, marshes, and a tidal stream. This segment is one of the Shoreline Greenway Trail's most active, and trail advocates, academic institutions, and environmental organizations utilize it to promote trail use and awareness throughout the neighboring communities.

CONTACT: shorelinegreenwaytrail.org

DIRECTIONS

East Haven: A parking lot is available at the corner of Hoop Pole Lane and Mansfield Grove Road.

To reach the trailhead from New Haven, take I-95 N to Exit 51 for US 1. Continue on US 1/ Frontage Road 1.4 miles and take a right onto Hemingway Ave. Go 1 mile south and turn left onto CT 142, which is also labeled Short Beach Road. Drive 0.7 mile and turn right onto Mansfield Grove Road. Continue 0.4 mile, then turn right onto Hoop Pole Lane. The parking lot is immediately on your left.

Branford: Parking for the Trolley Trail is offered at both ends: at Tilcon Road and off Thimble Island Road. To reach the Tilcon Road entrance from I-95, take Exit 55 for US 1 N/East Main St. Travel 0.3 mile on US 1 N, then make a right turn onto Featherbed Lane. Travel south 0.9 mile and take a left onto Damascus Road. In 0.2 mile, the road splits; veer right to get on Totoket Road. Continue on Totoket 1.1 miles, then take a left onto Tilcon Road. In 0.2 mile, the parking lot will be on your left.

To reach the Thimble Island Road entrance, from I-95 N, take Exit 56 for Leetes Island Road. Turn right onto Leetes Island Road in Branford and travel south 1.5 miles. At the three-way intersection, continue straight as the road becomes Thimble Island Road. After 0.5 mile, turn right on an undesignated street after passing Ridge Road (on the left). Continue down this street 0.1 mile to reach the parking lot. From I-95 S, take Exit 56, and turn left onto Industrial Road. In 0.3 mile turn left onto Leetes Island Road and follow the directions above.

Madison: From I-95, take Exit 62. Head south on Hammonasset Connector/CT 450. Travel 1.4 miles and make a right turn into the parking lot for Hammonasset Beach State Park.

Coming in at just under 3 miles, the Sue Grossman Still River Greenway is anchored by the towns of Winchester to the north and Torrington to the south. It occupies the right-of-way of the Naugatuck Division of the New York, New Haven and Hartford Railroad. Locomotives once hauled freight and carried passengers between Bridgeport and Winsted (an unincorporated community within Winchester). Following a slow decline in demand, rail service was discontinued in 1958 and the stretch between Torrington and Winsted was left fallow. The current incarnation of the Naugatuck Division offers seasonal themed excursions that run from Waterbury to Winsted.

At the Winchester trailhead, a ribbon of smooth, flat asphalt cuts through riparian wetland, with the Still River gliding quietly behind a screen of bushes and colorful wildflowers. Just before the intersection with Pinewoods

Watch for deer and rabbits among the trees and brush that line the path.

County
Litchfield

Endpoints
18 Lanson Dr., off Torrington Road (Winchester), to 2 Harris Dr., off Winsted Road (Torrington)

Mileage
2.9

Type
Rail-Trail

Roughness Index
1

Surface
Asphalt

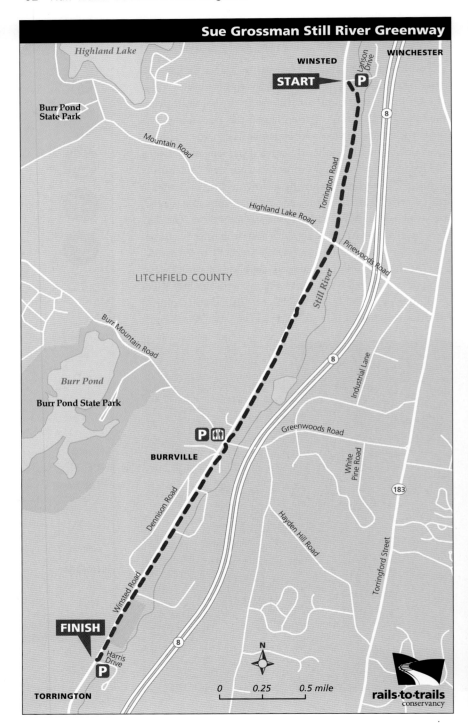

Road, you will see a trailside kiosk and memorial plaque. Benches here and at intervals along the way provide respite. Crossings are well marked, but they are at grade so use caution.

About a mile in, the trail begins to parallel Winsted Road, although the wall of wetland flora continues on your left, sandwiching the trail user between nature and civilization. Another 0.75 mile brings you to the Greenwoods Road intersection, past which you will find yourself in the tiny village of Burrville. There are a couple more minor road crossings before the trail terminates at the Harris Drive trailhead in Torrington.

Young and old alike will enjoy this scenic, family-friendly trail. Even if you go solo, don't be surprised if you have company; bunnies are a common sight and source of delight along the path. In your peripheral vision, you might catch a deer loping into the cover of trees in the surrounding protected lands. Perhaps the only downside to the Sue Grossman Still River Greenway is that it's relatively short, but even that is bound to change with planned extensions into downtown Winsted and Torrington.

CONTACT: torringtonct.org/parks-department/pages/trails

DIRECTIONS

To reach the northern trailhead from I-84, take Exit 20 and merge onto CT 8 toward Torrington. Continue on CT 8 for 21.3 miles, then take Exit 45 to Kennedy Road. Make a left onto Kennedy, followed in 0.2 mile by a right turn onto Winsted Road. Go 4 miles on Winsted Road to where it crosses the town line into Winchester and turns into Torrington Road. Stay on Torrington Road 0.5 mile and then turn right onto Lanson Dr. The trailhead will be on your right.

To reach the southern trailhead in Torrington from I-84, take Exit 20 and merge onto CT 8 toward Torrington. Continue on CT 8 for 21.3 miles, then take Exit 45 to Kennedy Road. Make a left onto Kennedy, followed in 0.2 mile by a right turn onto Winsted Road. Go 1.6 miles north and turn right onto Harris Dr.

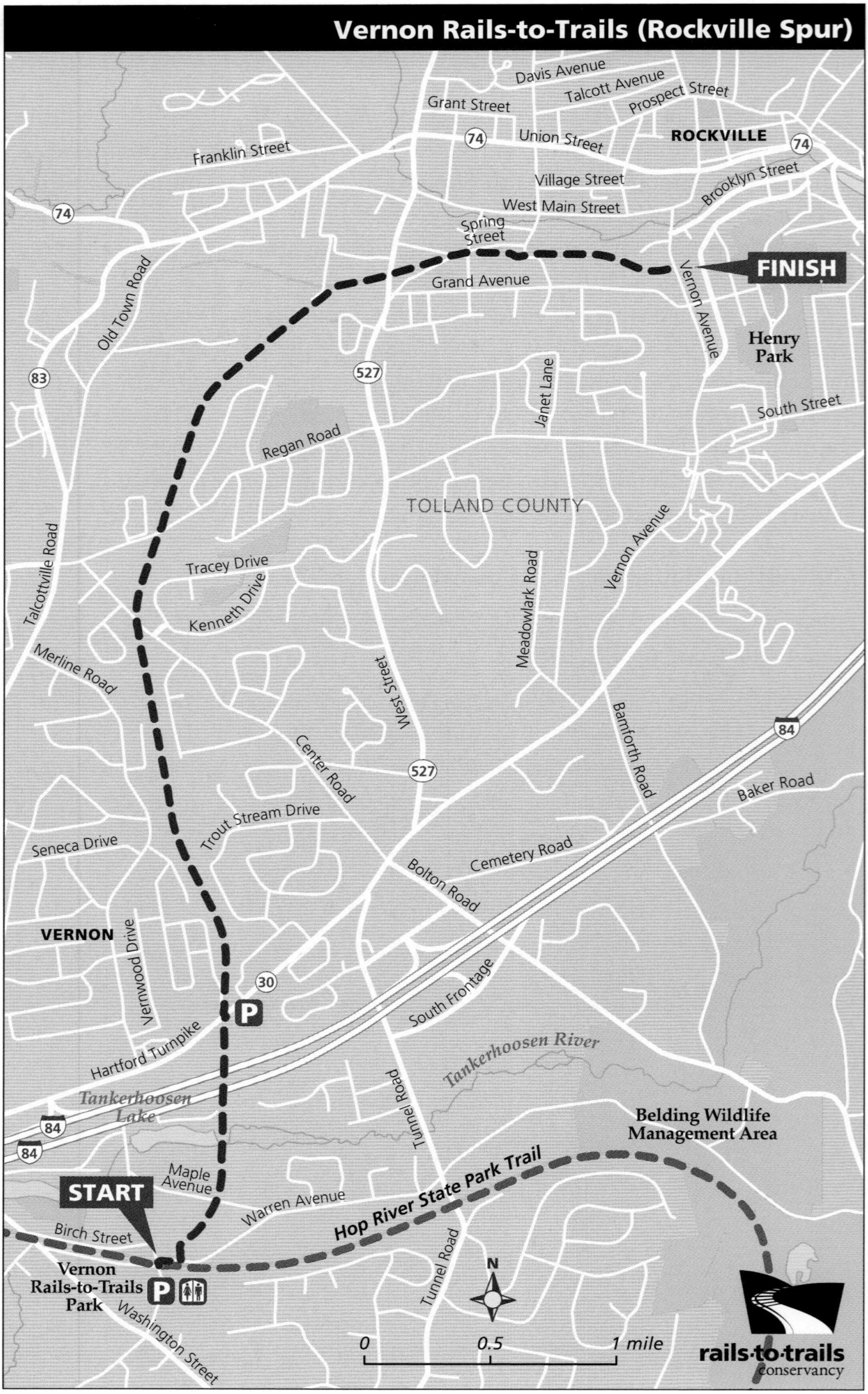

Vernon Rails-to-Trails (Rockville Spur)

Davis Avenue

Grant Street

Talcott Avenue

Prospect Street

Franklin Street

74

Union Street

ROCKVILLE

74

Village Street

West Main Street

Brooklyn Street

74

Spring Street

Grand Avenue

Vernon Avenue

FINISH

Old Town Road

83

527

Henry Park

Janet Lane

South Street

Regan Road

TOLLAND COUNTY

Talcottville Road

Tracey Drive

Vernon Avenue

Kenneth Drive

Merline Road

West Street

Meadowlark Road

Bamforth Road

84

Center Road

527

Baker Road

Seneca Drive

Trout Stream Drive

Cemetery Road

Bolton Road

VERNON

Vernwood Drive

30

P

South Frontage

Hartford Turnpike

Tankerhoosen River

Tankerhoosen Lake

84

Tunnel Road

Belding Wildlife Management Area

84

Maple Avenue

Warren Avenue

Hop River State Park Trail

START

Birch Street

Vernon Rails-to-Trails Park

P

Washington Street

Tunnel Road

N

0   0.5   1 mile

rails·to·trails
conservancy

Rockville Spur, a section of Vernon Rails-to-Trails, is a stone-dust rail-trail stretching 4.2 miles into the heart of historical Rockville. The trail begins on Warren Avenue in Vernon, but you'll probably start your journey 0.2 mile away, at the Vernon Rails-to-Trails Park on Church Street. The park was once the site of a train depot and today serves as the trailhead for Vernon's rail-trails, including the Rockville Spur. At this outdoor museum, panels tell the story of the Hartford, Providence & Fishkill Railroad, and remnants of the railroad bring the history to life. It's here, for example, that you'll learn that the Rockville Spur was constructed in 1863 to serve Rockville's once booming textile industry.

Once you've parked and sufficiently immersed yourself in history, it's time to go. To get to the trail's actual start point, just head west to Church Street's intersection with

At the I-84 underpass, you'll find murals painted by both local artists and schoolchildren.

County
Tolland

Endpoints
Hop River State Park Trail at Warren Ave. and Phoenix St. (Vernon) to Vernon Ave. between Brooklyn St. and Grand Ave. (Rockville)

Mileage
4.2

Type
Rail-Trail

Roughness Index
1

Surfaces
Crushed Stone, Dirt

Phoenix Street. Make a left onto Phoenix and then take the first right—that's Warren Avenue. A signpost marks the beginning of the trail, and markers every 0.25 mile guide you along the way. Note that if you're up for more riding at the end of your journey, you can pick up another trail from the park: the 20-mile Hop River State Park Trail (see page 26).

Once you're on the spur, you'll exchange the suburban scene for a serene wooded corridor. At about 0.25 mile, you'll come to the Maple Avenue intersection, the first crossing of several along this trail. Each intersection may require patience because there are crosswalks but no signals.

Once you're across this street and back on the trail, you will come to one of the trail highlights: the bridge over the scenic Tankerhoosen River. This waterway was the economic lifeblood of Rockville during the town's industrial heyday. The view upriver, with trees crowding its banks, is Tankerhoosen Lake, one of seven ponds on the river. It's worth pausing your journey at this point to take it all in. Continuing on, you will come to the I-84 underpass, the only road crossing not at grade. In the space between the tunnels, you'll find another treat: murals bursting with color on the walls, the work of local artists and schoolchildren.

The next intersection is across the busy CT 30 (Hartford Turnpike). The trail continues through the woods with unmarked paths feeding into it from nearby homes, proof of how popular this trail is with local residents. At the 3.25-mile mark (West Street), you'll notice that the trail narrows into little more than a swath in the grass as it emerges into a residential neighborhood. Half a mile later, you'll find yourself back in the woods where the path opens up again. Just shy of Vernon Avenue, the spur ends abruptly on an earthen mound atop an old bridge abutment. You can either retrace your steps back, or use the path on your left to go down the embankment (be careful; the soil is loose) onto Vernon Avenue.

CONTACT: vernonct.com/trails.htm

DIRECTIONS

To reach the Church St. trailhead in Vernon, from I-84 E, take Exit 65 for CT 30 toward Vernon Center. Turn right onto CT 30, and in 0.2 mile turn right onto Dobson Road, which turns into Washington St. After 0.4 mile, make a slight left onto Church St. The Vernon Rails-to-Trails Park will be on your left and includes a parking area, benches and picnic tables, and the outdoor museum. From I-84 W, take Exit 65 and turn left onto CT 30. In 0.3 mile turn left onto Dobson Road and follow the directions above from there.

The Windsor Locks Canal State Park Trail occupies a narrow strip of land between the Connecticut River and the eponymous canal. Also known as the Enfield Falls Canal, the waterway opened in 1829, allowing boats to avoid shallow water along this stretch of the adjacent river. Now operated as a state park, the paved trail replaced the towpath once used by mules and their human drivers to tow freight along the canal until the system was rendered obsolete by railroads in the mid- to late 19th century.

The trail's isolation between two waterways, as well as its abundant vegetation, makes it the perfect place to spot wildlife. The natural beauty and tranquility, coupled with its convenience to large population centers in both Connecticut and Massachusetts, make the trail a popular destination, and you'll likely run into scores of happy trail users no matter the day. Families, many with leashed dogs,

Tucked between two waterways and surrounded by abundant vegetation, the pathway is the ideal place to spot wildlife.

County
Hartford

Endpoints
East St. N/CT 159 and Franklin St./CT 190 (Suffield) and Pearl St. and Franklin St./CT 190 (Enfield) to Bridge St./ CT 140 and Main St./ CT 159 at the Connecticut River (Windsor Locks)

Mileage
5.4

Type
Canal

Roughness Index
1

Surface
Asphalt

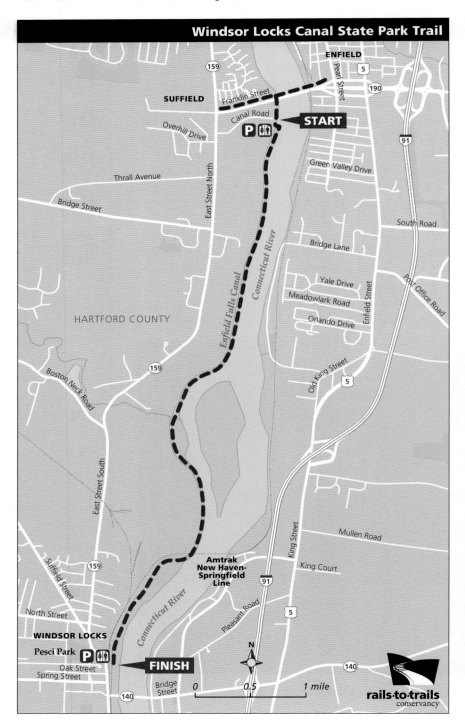

Windsor Locks Canal State Park Trail

are particularly abundant. A short segment of the route built more recently extends the trail over the CT 190 bridge to the east, providing nonmotorized access to residents of Enfield and no doubt increasing the trail's use even more.

Begin your journey in the north at a large parking lot at the end of Canal Road in Suffield. Shortly after you start heading south, you're forced to navigate a narrow footbridge over the canal. Carefully avoid the fishermen who are almost guaranteed to be plying their craft—indeed, you'll often see cyclists riding down the trail with rods slung over their shoulders en route to their favorite fishing spot—and you'll enter the comfortable shade of the official towpath.

The scenic, well-used path is a straight shot south, giving you ample opportunities to take in expansive views of the Connecticut River to your left. Do keep your eyes on the pavement, though: aggressive tree roots pushing up the asphalt can make for a bumpy ride, while the many geese who lay claim to the trail don't like to clean up after themselves. Occasionally, you'll spot old stonework that will remind you of the canal's rich history.

Closer to the trail's southern end, you'll pass under Amtrak's active New Haven–Springfield Line, which crosses the Connecticut River here—making the trail an ideal vantage point for railfans. Shortly thereafter, you'll end at a nondescript parking lot and traversable gate intended to prevent cars from accessing the trail. The lot is located behind a vacant factory, one of many that once used water from the canal to power its mills after the waterway's transportation use ceased. Continue down the paved access road behind the building to reach CT 140 and nearby civic facilities in Windsor Locks, or head back the way you came to return to your car.

Per state rules, the trail is open only April 1–November 15, 30 minutes before sunrise to 30 minutes after sunset.

CONTACT: www.ct.gov/deep/windsorlockscanaltrail

DIRECTIONS

To reach the northern trailhead in Suffield from I-91, take Exit 47W, then head west (right) on CT 190 toward Suffield. Shortly after you cross the Connecticut River (1.4 miles in all), turn left onto CT 159/East St. N. Next, take the first left onto Canal Road. Go 0.4 mile on Canal Road to its end at the trailhead parking lot.

To reach the southern trailhead in Windsor Locks from I-91, take Exit 42 for CT 159 toward Windsor Locks, then turn left onto S. Main St. After a little more than a mile, turn right onto CT 140/Bridge St. Take a left behind the vacant factory building, immediately after you cross the canal but before you cross the Connecticut River. The access road ends shortly thereafter at the trailhead parking lot.

rails-to-trails conservancy

Shining Sea Bikeway.............. 44
Southwest Corridor Park
(Pierre Lallement Bike Path)...... 45
Upper Charles Trail.............. 46

16 Amesbury Riverwalk..............
17 Ashuwillticook Rail Trail..........
18 Assabet River Rail Trail...........
19 Border to Boston Trail............
20 Bridge of Flowers...............
21 Bruce Freeman Rail Trail..........
22 Canalside Rail Trail.............
23 Cape Cod Canal Bikeway..........
24 Cape Cod Rail Trail.............
25 Charles River Bike Path..........
26 Clipper City Rail Trail
   and Harborwalk..............
27 Columbia Greenway Rail Trail
   and Southwick Rail Trail.........
28 East Boston Greenway...........
29 Grand Trunk Trail...............
30 Independence Greenway..........
31 Manhan Rail Trail...............
32 Marblehead Rail-Trail/
   Salem Bike Path..............
33 Mass Central Rail Trail...........
34 Minuteman Bikeway............
35 Narrow-Gauge Rail-Trail..........
36 Nashua River Rail Trail...........
37 Neponset River Greenway.........
38 North Central Pathway..........
39 Northern Strand
   Community Trail..............
40 Old Colony Rail Trail............
41 Phoenix Bike Trail..............
42 Province Lands Bike Trail.........
43 Reformatory Branch Trail..........

ATLANTIC OCEAN

VERMONT

NEW HAMPSHIRE

MASSACHUSETTS

CONNECTICUT

RHODE ISLAND

ATLANTIC OCEAN

Manchester
Gloucester
Boston
Lowell
Quincy
Nashua
Brattleboro
Greenfield
Pittsfield
Northampton
Springfield
Worcester
Hartford
Providence
Newport
Plymouth
Provincetown
Barnstable
New Bedford
Cape Cod
Cape Cod Bay
Nantucket
Martha's Vineyard

N

0 10 20 30 miles

Massachusetts

Charles River Bike Path (see page 91)

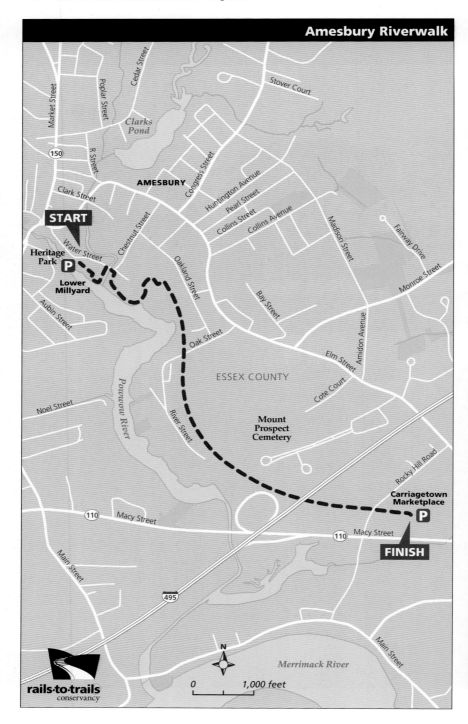

Amesbury Riverwalk

The Amesbury Riverwalk (also known as the Powwow Riverwalk) carries visitors between a resurgent waterfront district on the Powwow River to a modern shopping center on the outskirts of this historical mill town. The 1.3-mile paved trail is part of the Coastal Trails Network, which one day will link several northeastern Massachusetts communities with 30 miles of trail.

The trail follows the Amesbury-Salisbury branch of the coastal Eastern Railroad that began serving the area in 1848. The rival Boston and Maine Railroad took over in 1884 and ran the line until 1972. The city of Amesbury and Coastal Trails Coalition created the trail in 1999.

Beginning a trail tour at Heritage Park in the Lower Millyard introduces you to the city's history as a 19th- and early-20th-century manufacturing center. A parking lot in this redeveloped area provides access to the trail and Heritage Park, as well as to restaurants and pubs in the area.

Although civilization is close at hand, much of the trail is tucked into the trees.

County
Essex

Endpoints
Heritage Park on Water St. between Ring St. and Chestnut St. to Carriagetown Marketplace on Macy St. between Rocky Hill Road and Elm St. (Amesbury)

Mileage
1.3

Type
Rail-Trail

Roughness Index
1

Surface
Asphalt

Here on the Powwow River (a tributary of the Merrimack River), industrialists in the 1800s built a series of dams to harness the river's power for textile mills. Later on, carriage-making took over as the dominant industry, lending its identity to Amesbury's nickname, Carriagetown. A fire destroyed many of those buildings in 1888, but the carriage industry roared back, shifting to automobile bodies until the Great Depression.

Old multistory brick buildings next to Heritage Park housed mill and carriage operations but are being repurposed to other uses. Upon first entering the park from Water Street, you'll see the small Salisbury Point Station, which was built in the 1870s by the Eastern Railroad and relocated here.

Winding through the park, the trail overlooks the Powwow River before an interruption for a bridge across Back River on Water Street. (Use the crosswalk to reach the sidewalk on the north side of the bridge, then cross Water Street again to return to the trail.) The trail rolls alongside the river then beneath Oak Street, where it enters a wooded area that surrounds the aged Mount Prospect Cemetery. Here you'll find the final resting place of *Li'l Abner* cartoonist Al Capp, among others.

Passing underneath I-495 and crossing Rocky Hill Road, the trail ends at the Carriagetown Marketplace, a shopping center where you'll find many opportunities for food and refreshment. The Coastal Trails Coalition is working with local and state agencies to finish a trail network linking Amesbury, Salisbury, Newbury, and Newburyport via the Salisbury Point Ghost Trail (less than a mile away), the Old Eastern Marsh Trail, Clipper City Rail Trail (see page 95), and the Plum Island bike lanes.

CONTACT: coastaltrails.org and **amesburyma.gov/home/pages/amesbury-riverwalk**

DIRECTIONS

To reach the western trailhead at Heritage Park from I-95, take Exit 58 (from the north) or Exit 58B (from the south) toward MA 110 W and Amesbury. Head west on MA 110/Macy St. for about 0.2 mile, and turn right onto Elm St. Go 1.3 miles and turn left onto Chestnut St., and then go 0.2 mile and turn right onto County Road/Water St. Go 0.1 mile and turn right into a parking lot. The trailhead is across Water St. in Heritage Park.

To reach the eastern trailhead at Carriagetown Marketplace from I-95, take Exit 58 (from the north) or Exit 58B (from the south) toward MA 110 W and Amesbury. Head west on MA 110/Macy St. 0.4 mile, and turn right into Carriagetown Marketplace at the traffic signal. Go about 300 feet and turn left and then right to access the rear of the shopping center. Parking and the trailhead are on the left.

Visitors to the Ashuwillticook Rail Trail will find the full splendor of the scenic Berkshires along this nearly 12-mile-long paved trail. The Ashuwillticook (ash-oo-will-tī-cook) follows MA 8 through the Hoosic River valley between Lanesborough and Adams while providing views of mountains, lakes, and rivers, as well as turning leaves in autumn.

The trail owes its existence to the Pittsfield and North Adams Railroad, which sought to extend the Housatonic Railroad from Pittsfield, Massachusetts, to Rutland, Vermont, in the 1840s. The Western Railroad acquired the line before its completion, and it was later operated by the Boston & Albany Railroad, the New York Central, and finally the Boston and Maine Railroad. The corridor became disused in 1990, and local residents gained support for a multiuse trail. It opened in three phases in 2001, 2004, and 2017.

The route starts at a trailhead in Lanesborough on the outskirts of Pittsfield, a manufacturing center of the late 19th and early 20th centuries. Consider packing a picnic

Skirting the Cheshire Reservoir is a highlight of the route.

County
Berkshire

Endpoints
US 7/MA 8 Connector Road between MA 8 and Partridge Road (Lanesborough) to Lime St. between Print Works Dr. and Columbia St. (Adams)

Mileage
11.9

Type
Rail-Trail

Roughness Index
1

Surface
Asphalt

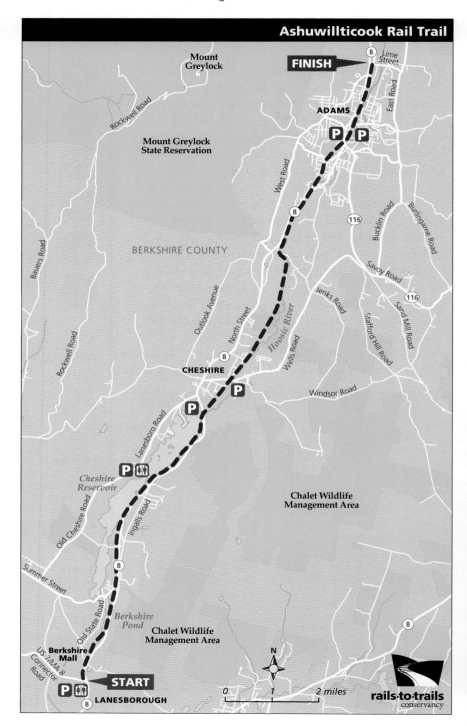

lunch, so you can relax and see the sights along the trail. Although there are food stops, most are on the wrong side of a busy state highway.

The trail rolls into the woods between the tranquil Hoosic River and MA 8, which is screened from the path by trees. You'll pass Berkshire Pond in the first mile before arriving at the 418-acre Cheshire Reservoir, created in the 1860s to provide power for area textile mills. Along its 2.4-mile trailside shoreline, you might see anglers casting for bass, northern pike, and yellow perch. Keep your eyes open for ospreys and herons, as well as turtles sunning themselves on logs. You'll have an unobstructed view of Mount Greylock, the highest point in the state, across the lake.

You can find snacks and refreshments in Cheshire at the north end of the reservoir; an old Boston & Albany Railroad station houses a business next to the trail. The remaining 4 miles to the edge of Adams passes wood lots and farms.

The area's manufacturing history unfolds as you arrive in Adams and see old mill buildings on the far shore of the Hoosic River. The route parallels the town's restored main street that boasts quaint stores and eateries. Archways and banners throughout Adams sport a black bear riding a bicycle, a nod to both the trail and the resident black bear population. The old passenger station still stands at 10 Pleasant Street, and parking is available at the visitor center (3 Hoosac Street).

A trail segment that opened in 2017 rolls north 1.1 miles to Lime Street in the vicinity of a lime mining and production facility that dates to the 1840s. Future extensions north to North Adams and south into Pittsfield are in the planning stage.

CONTACT: mass.gov/locations/ashuwillticook-rail-trail

DIRECTIONS

To reach the Lanesborough trailhead from I-90, take Exit 2 to the toll plaza and bear right onto US 20/Housatonic St. toward Pittsfield. In 0.7 mile turn right onto Main St. Go 0.4 mile, and turn slightly left to remain on US 20 W. Go 10.2 miles and turn right in Pittsfield onto MA 9/East St. toward Dalton/Northampton. Go 1.4 miles and continue straight onto Merrill Road, and then go 1.8 miles and bear left onto MA 8/Cheshire Road. Go 1.5 miles and turn left onto US 7/MA 8 Connector Road. Parking is on the left and the right after the turn.

To reach the Adams trailhead, follow the directions above to MA 8/Cheshire Road. Go 12.1 miles north on MA 8/Cheshire Road, and turn left onto Center St./Park St. In 0.3 mile, turn right onto Hoosac St., and then take an immediate right onto Depot St.

To reach the Adams trailhead from the intersection of MA 2 and MA 8 in North Adams, head south on MA 8/State St. Go 5.5 miles and turn left onto Hoosac St. Take an immediate right onto Depot St. Parking is on the left. Cross Hoosac St. and continue 1.2 miles north to reach the endpoint on Lime St.

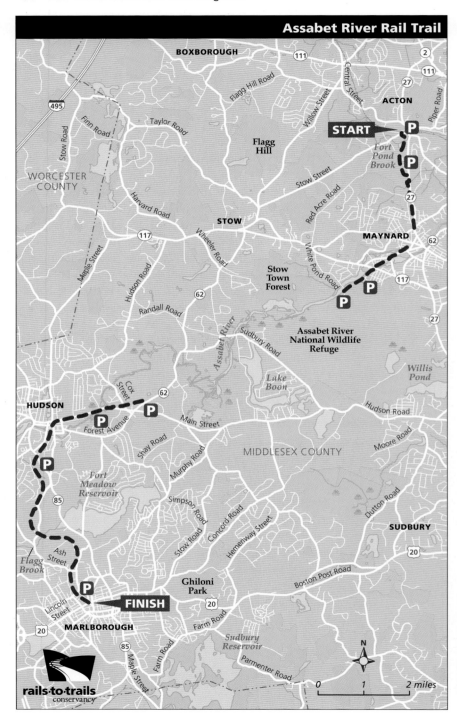

The Assabet River Rail Trail connects five old mill towns that owe their revitalization to present-day high-tech industries. A midpoint gap splits the 8.6-mile paved trail, though long-range plans call for a 12.5-mile trail from Acton; through Maynard, Stow, and Hudson; to Marlborough. It offers a forested escape for recreation and a route for Boston-bound bike commuters to reach the train station in South Acton.

Trail plans date to 1992, when local residents eyed the former railbed of the Marlborough Branch Railroad as a rail-trail project. The branch ran from a junction with the main line Fitchburg Railroad in Acton

A restored 1921 Boston and Maine Railroad caboose sits trailside in Hudson.

County
Middlesex

Endpoints
Maple St. and Stow St. (Acton) to White Pond Road between Shore Ave. and Taylor Road (Maynard); and MA 62/ Wilkins St., 250 feet northeast of Orchard St (Hudson), to Lincoln St. at Highland St. and Cashman St. (Marlborough)

Mileage
8.6

Type
Rail-Trail

Roughness Index
1

Surface
Asphalt

southward along the Assabet River beginning in 1849, extending to Marlborough by 1855. The Fitchburg Railroad subsequently merged with Boston and Maine Railroad. Passenger service ended in 1958; freight ended in the 1960s. All five towns along the route voted in support of the rail-trail in 1998, and the first section opened in 2005.

The newest section of paved trail starts opposite the tracks of the Massachusetts Bay Transportation Authority's (MBTA) South Acton Station; passengers can take bicycles on the Fitchburg line on Saturdays, Sundays, and off-peak hours during the week. Dedicated trail parking is available on Maple Street.

Starting in Acton, you'll pass the only farm along the trail on the right, and then cross the Fort Pond Brook, which attracted mills here beginning in the early 1700s. The trail enters wetlands before arriving in Maynard and traveling through its busy downtown. You'll cross the Assabet River here on a bridge installed in 2017 and get good views of renovated 19th-century mill buildings.

The paved rail-trail ends at White Pond Road at mile 3.2. For the next 1.9 miles the railroad corridor passes through the 2,230-acre Assabet River National Wildlife Refuge on Track Road, a public access dirt road that's more suitable for mountain bikes. The next 2 miles of corridor, between Sudbury Road and the trailhead on MA 62/Wilkins Street in Hudson, is closed, as it crosses private land.

You'll regain the older section of rail-trail at the MA 62 trailhead, roughly where a future section of the Mass Central Rail Trail (see page 118) will cross on its 23-mile route from Berlin to Waltham. You'll get a good look at the Assabet River as you cross a small bridge alongside MA 62/Main Street, then you'll see a restored 1921 Boston and Maine Railroad blue caboose before you enter Hudson's commercial district. Hudson was once known as Shoe Town for all the shoe-making factories along the river. The best view of the river comes about 0.6 mile past the caboose as you cross a trestle 40 feet above the river.

Leaving Hudson, the trail again plunges into woods that offer a shady canopy as you begin a gentle climb to Marlborough. Passing beneath MA 85, you enter Marlborough and cross wetlands around Flagg Brook that serves as a wildlife corridor. You can see the Fort Meadow Reservoir from an overlook with benches. The path continues about another mile, reaching the trail high point at Hudson Street, before ending on Lincoln Street.

CONTACT: arrtinc.org

DIRECTIONS

To reach the Acton trailhead from I-495, take Exit 28 to MA 111 W/Massachusetts Ave. Head 3.7 miles west on MA 111/Massachusetts Ave., and turn right onto Central St. Go 1.5 miles and bear right onto MA 27/Main St. Go 0.1 mile and turn right onto Maple St. Trailhead parking is 0.1 mile on the left.

To reach the Ice House Landing trailhead in Maynard from I-495, take Exit 27 to MA 117 W/Main St./Great Road. Head 5.2 miles west on MA 117, and go straight to join MA 62/MA 117/Great Road. Go another 2.2 miles and turn right onto Winter St., then go 0.2 mile and look for the Ice House Landing trailhead on the right.

To reach the Hudson trailhead parking from I-495, take Exit 26 toward Hudson on MA 62/Coolidge St. Go 2.0 miles east and take the second exit off the roundabout to follow MA 62/Main St. Go 1.6 miles and turn left onto MA 62/Wilkins St. Look for trailhead parking on the left in 0.3 mile.

To reach parking in Marlborough from I-495, take Exit 24A toward US 20 E/Lakeside Ave. Go 0.8 mile east and turn left onto US 20/W. Main St. Go 0.5 mile and turn left onto Winthrop St., then go 0.2 mile and turn right onto Lincoln St. Go 0.1 mile and turn left onto Mechanic St., then go 0.2 mile and turn right onto Hudson St. Look for parking in 0.1 mile on the left just past the trail. The trail ends 0.3 mile to the south.

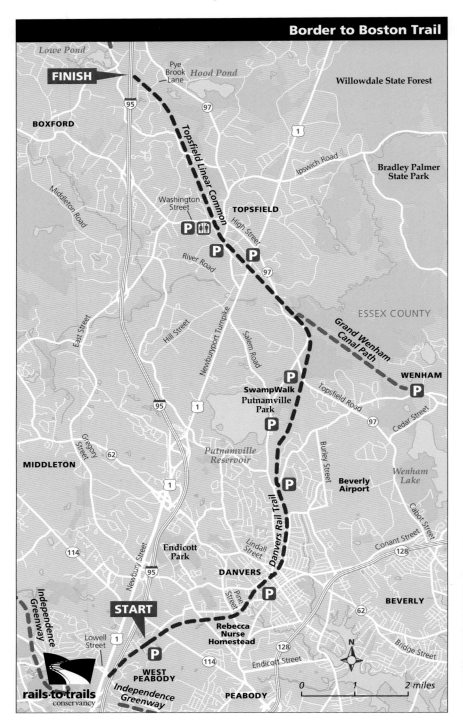

Border to Boston Trail

Lowe Pond

FINISH

Pye Brook Lane

Hood Pond

Willowdale State Forest

95

97

BOXFORD

1

Ipswich Road

Bradley Palmer State Park

Middleton Road

Washington Street

Topsfield Linear Common

TOPSFIELD

High Street

River Road

P

P

P

97

ESSEX COUNTY

East Street

Hill Street

Newburyport Turnpike

Salem Road

Grand Wenham Canal Path

WENHAM

P

95

1

SwampWalk Putnamville Park

P

P

Topsfield Road

97

Cedar Street

Gregory Street

62

MIDDLETON

1

Putnamville Reservoir

Burley Street

Beverly Airport

Wenham Lake

P

Cabot Street

114

Newbury Street

95

Endicott Park

Lindall Street

Danvers Rail Trail

DANVERS

Conant Street

128

BEVERLY

62

P

START

Pine Street

Independence Greenway

Lowell Street

1

P

WEST PEABODY

Rebecca Nurse Homestead

114

Endicott Street

128

Bridge Street

N

rails-to-trails conservancy

Independence Greenway

PEABODY

0   1   2 miles

The Border to Boston Trail connects the communities of West Peabody, Peabody, Danvers, Topsfield, and Boxford in northeastern Massachusetts. The long-term goal for the trail is to continue it north to the New Hampshire border and south to the Boston suburbs, hence the trail's name. When complete, the trail will span 28 miles.

The railroad that originally served the corridor from Peabody to Topsfield was built in the 1850s. It provided passenger service until 1959 and freight service until 1977. The corridor lay dormant until construction of the trail began in 2006, and it now serves as part of the East Coast Greenway, a connected network of trails that, when complete, will stretch from Maine to Florida.

Starting on its southern end at the border between Peabody and Danvers, this section of the Border to Boston Trail is known locally as the Danvers Rail Trail. Heading northeast, you will enjoy a quiet, somewhat wooded journey in a suburban atmosphere along a crushed-stone pathway dotted with wildflowers.

Topsfield Linear Common, the northern section of the trail, offers a wooded and secluded experience.

County
Essex County

Endpoints
Lowell St., 0.1 mile northwest of Bourbon St. (Peabody), to Pye Brook Lane, just northeast of Perkins Way (Boxford)

Mileage
10.7

Type
Rail-Trail

Roughness Index
1–2

Surfaces
Crushed Stone, Dirt

After riding 1.3 miles, you will come to Pine Street; if you turn right here and travel one block, you can visit the historical Rebecca Nurse Homestead and a reproduction of the Salem Village Meetinghouse to learn about the Salem witch trials. Rebecca Nurse was found guilty of witchcraft and hanged in 1692. The home and meetinghouse are open May–November.

From Pine Street, you have another 3.3 miles of riding before your next major attraction, the SwampWalk. Dismount if riding and enjoy a 0.3-mile stroll across boardwalks that take you on an immersive journey into the heart of the Wenham Great Swamp. Keep your eyes peeled for turtles, frogs, ducks, fox, deer, and turkeys. The horseshoe-shaped SwampWalk will deposit you back on the main trail.

Continue north and cross the Topsfield border, where the trail segment is now called the Topsfield Linear Common. In 1.3 miles from the SwampWalk, you'll see an opportunity to hop on another trail off to the right. The 2-mile Grand Wenham Canal Path offers a scenic and peaceful side excursion along a canal built in 1917. Note that the Topsfield section permits equestrian use, though the Danvers section does not.

North of Wenham Road, the suburban trail transitions to a more wooded and secluded experience, and you'll come across hiking trails that connect to the main trail. After crossing Washington Street, you only have 2.4 miles to go. In this final leg, the width of the path narrows and the surface becomes packed dirt, so this section is better suited for bikes with wider tires. The trail ultimately dead-ends as it approaches I-95.

CONTACTS: danversrailtrail.org and **topsfieldtrail.org**

DIRECTIONS

The starting point on Lowell St. does not have parking. To reach Danvers Indoor Sports, which offers the nearest parking spot to the trail's southern end, take I-95 S to Exit 50 and merge onto US 1 S/Newbury St./Newburyport Turnpike. In 2.8 miles exit onto MA 114 E/Andover St. toward Peabody. Head 0.5 mile east on MA 114, and turn right onto the unnamed street before the gas station. Danvers Indoor Sports is in the back of the commercial complex. Access the trail by going behind the building. The beginning of the trail is less than a mile away from the parking lot. From I-95 N, take Exit 47A for MA 114, and head 0.5 mile east. Turn right onto the unnamed street before the gas station, and follow the directions above to access the trail.

There is no parking at the northern endpoint either. The closest parking is available on Park St. between Main St. and Summer St., 2.5 miles from the trail's terminus. To reach the parking lot from I-95, take Exit 50, and head north on US 1. In 2.4 miles, turn left onto S. Main St., and go 0.6 mile. Turn right onto Summer St. From Newbury head south on US 1 about 10 miles, and turn right onto High St. In 0.2 mile turn left onto Summer St. The trail and the parking lot will be on your left.

The Bridge of Flowers delights the senses of visitors walking among the trees and blossoms on the old trolley bridge spanning the Deerfield River, which connects two communities in northwestern Massachusetts: Shelburne Falls and Buckland. The 400-foot concrete bridge comes alive every year April 1–October 30 as a garden pathway with flowering plants of all varieties.

The closed-spandrel deck arch bridge originally carried trolley cars between Shelburne Falls and Buckland on the Shelburne Falls & Colrain Street Railway from 1908 until 1927, when the railroad folded. The bridge remained, however, as it also carried a water main between the two towns. The bridge was in danger of becoming a weedy eyesore, so the Shelburne Falls Area Women's Club took on the task of beautifying the bridge in 1929. Its volunteers have been planting flowers and maintaining the flower beds on the bridge ever since.

Although the bridge deck is 18 feet wide, the pathway is much narrower with the lush garden on both sides. Walkers are encouraged, but bicycles and pets—even those you can carry—are prohibited. The bridge is wheelchair accessible. If you're on a bike, you can cross the river on adjacent Bridge Street, which provides an excellent view of the Bridge of Flowers.

County
Franklin

Endpoints
State St. between
William St. and Bridge St.
(Buckland) to Water St.
between Cross St.
and Bridge St.
(Shelburne Falls)

Mileage
0.1

Type
Rail-Trail

Roughness Index
1

Surface
Concrete

Volunteers have been tending to the gardens along the bridge since 1929.

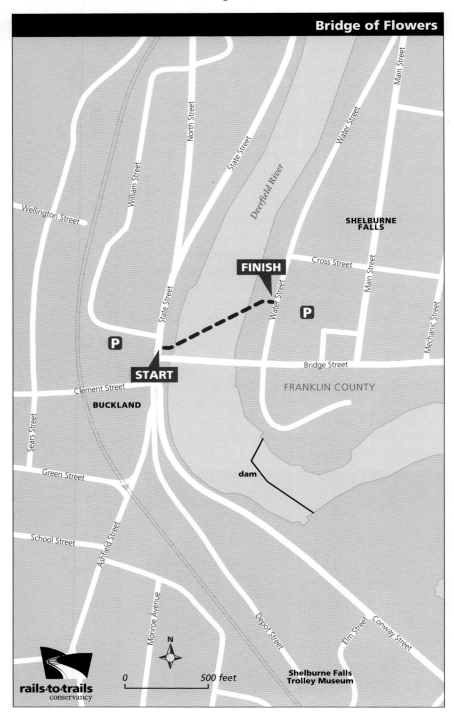

Bridge of Flowers

The closed-spandrel deck arch bridge originally carried the Shelburne Falls & Colrain Street Railway.

The bridge offers welcoming gardens at either end: State Street in Buckland and Water Street in Shelburne Falls. Following the path, flower lovers are greeted by an ever-changing variety of bulbs, perennials, shrubs, and trees that beg for attention. They range from crocus in the early spring to asters in the fall. Once it snows, the bridge is closed behind locked gates because of liability issues until spring.

As the main attraction, the bridge drew a collection of specialty shops, restaurants, bookstores, a coffee shop, and a soda fountain. Nearby is the Shelburne Falls Trolley Museum, home of car No. 10, the only surviving trolley car from the Shelburne Falls & Colrain Street Railway. Dating to 1896, it was rescued by a local farmer who used it as a chicken coop, toolshed, and playhouse for 65 years until the museum acquired it. Now it's used for rides around the old railway freight yard where the museum keeps other railroad and trolley artifacts.

CONTACT: bridgeofflowersmass.org

DIRECTIONS

To reach the west trailhead from I-91, take Exit 26 toward North Adams on MA 2 W/Mohawk Trail. Go 8.3 miles west and turn left onto S. Maple St. Go 0.3 mile and turn left onto Bridge St. In 0.5 mile turn right onto State St. after crossing the road bridge. Look for on-street parking or a parking lot on the right.

To reach the east trailhead from I-91, follow the directions above to Bridge St. In 0.3 mile turn right onto Main St. A municipal parking lot is on the left. The entrance to the Bridge of Flowers is across the parking lot on Water St.

The bridge is open April–October.

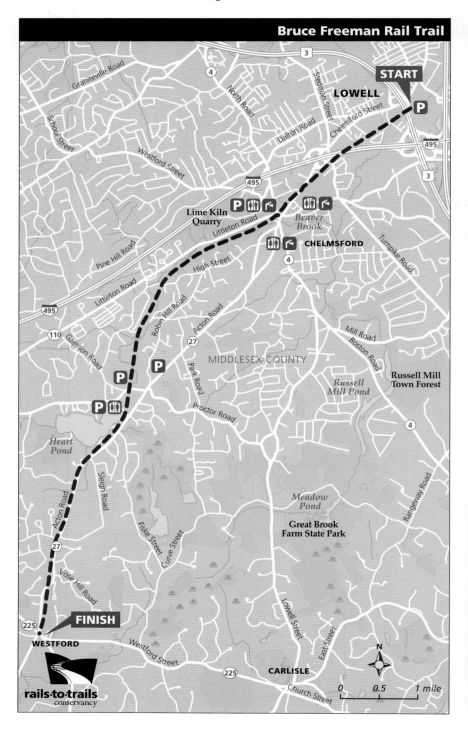

Bruce Freeman Rail Trail

Bruce N. Freeman was a Massachusetts state representative from 1969 to 1986. Beginning in 1985, he championed the creation of a bike path that would run along the former Penn Central railroad line from Industrial Avenue in Lowell to South Sudbury. Inspiration for the trail (then referred to as the Lowell-Sudbury Rail Trail) came partly from seeing the Cape Cod Rail Trail (see page 88), as well as a bike trail in San Jose, California, on which Freeman had ridden with his son and grandson. After Freeman's death in 1986, his successor Carol C. Cleven introduced a bill that would make the bike path a reality.

You'll want to start your journey at the northern endpoint in Lowell, as it is the only endpoint located near a parking lot. From here, a green painted path goes from the nearest building into the trail parking lot, providing great access for those who work in the buildings near the trailhead.

The trail offers a variety of scenery, ducking in and out of the trees and through residential and business areas.

County
Middlesex

Endpoints
Trail parking lot near 900 Chelmsford St. (Lowell) to MA 225/Westford St. and MA 27/Acton Road (Westford)

Mileage
6.8

Type
Rail-Trail

Roughness Index
1

Surface
Asphalt

The trail starts with an extensive culvert tunnel under US 3/Northwest Expressway. On the other side of the tunnel, you're greeted with flowers as the rail-trail runs along the back side of several business areas. In 0.8 mile from the trailhead, the trail runs diagonally under the large I-495/Blue Star Memorial Highway overpass as you enter the Chelmsford area. Baseball fields are just off the trail to the left as you cross Chelmsford Street in another 0.5 mile. The path begins again on the other side. Here, you'll make your way into a little downtown area, where the trail follows Chelmsford Street very briefly.

In 0.3 mile, be careful as you cross the central intersection of MA 4/North Road and MA 110/Littleton Road, as this is located in the middle of town. Take the trail almost straight through the intersection, following signs for the safe crosswalks that will lead you to the other side. A small lantern man sculpture off to the right lets you know that you're back on the trail. A few more pieces of art are just ahead, where an old train depot used to be.

As you head out of town for the remaining 5.1 miles, you'll pass through a rural section—much of it covered by tree canopies—following Beaver Brook as it makes its way through neighborhoods. This section of trail is leisurely and wide, with fencing along both sides in some portions. In 2.7 miles, to the right of the trail in Chelmsford, is Heart Pond. Note that the beach—which contains a playground and swimming area—is open to the public. The trail skips over the corner of Heart Pond and travels along a small dockside community. It then continues south through more wooded areas with portions of fencing along the trail, adding to the structural beauty of the corridor. In 2.4 miles from Heart Pond Beach, the trail ends rather abruptly at Westford Street, without parking or a trailhead sign of any sort. The county is currently extending the trail farther south, however, and a few people do venture along the dirt corridor walking or on mountain bikes.

CONTACT: brucefreemanrailtrail.org

DIRECTIONS

To reach the northern trailhead from I-495, take Exit 35A-35B to head north on US 3. In 0.1 mile take Exit 31, following signs for MA 110/Lowell/Chelmsford. Turn right onto MA 110 W./Chelmsford St., and almost immediately make a right into the office building complex. Follow the road to the parking lot and make a right just before crossing a brook. The trail has its own parking at the side of the lot, and a green painted path leads from the office building to the trailhead. The trail begins with a tunnel under the Northwest Expwy./US 3. There is no parking at the southern trailhead.

The well-maintained Canalside Rail Trail provides users with a variety of trestle bridges, views of waterbirds stalking fish and frogs, and gentle grades that alternate between open sky and forested shade. The majority of the trail lies within historic Turners Falls—the largest of the five villages that comprise the town of Montague.

From the public parking lot at Unity Park in Montague, begin your journey by turning left onto the paved trail, starting with views of the Connecticut River Reservoir and Turners Falls Dam to your right. You can also see the Turners Falls Fishway, composed of three fish ladders that enable fish to travel beyond the dam. The fish ladders are located at the Cabot Hydroelectric Station, the dam, and the gatehouse.

Once you cross Avenue A, you'll pass the Great Falls Discovery Center on your left. After this point, the trail parallels the canal for about 2 miles—crossing Turners Falls Road, Power Street, and 11th Street—and offers ample opportunities to see several small trestle bridges. The rail-trail takes a left onto Depot Street to leave the canal, making several turns through neighborhood streets and a light

A trestle bridge, built in 1880, is located near the confluence of the Connecticut and Deerfield Rivers on the southern end of the rail-trail.

County
Franklin

Endpoints
Unity Park at First St., 0.1 mile southeast of Williams Way (Montague), to McClelland Farm Road between River Road and Railroad Yard Road (Deerfield)

Mileage
3.6

Type
Rail-Trail

Roughness Index
1

Surface
Asphalt

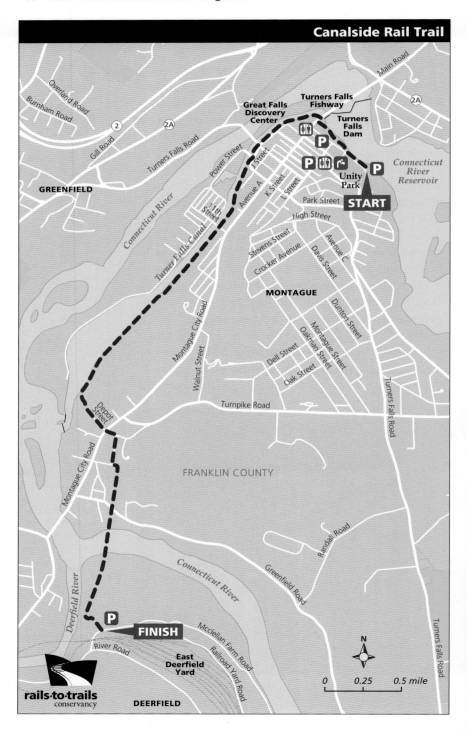

industry area, requiring users to travel on the public roadway for a short distance. Street traffic is light and the crossings are well marked, suitable for users of all ages.

In 0.4 mile, the path returns to dedicated foot and bike usage and leads to a gorgeous trestle bridge near the confluence of the Connecticut and Deerfield Rivers. The bridge was constructed in 1880, with sections repaired following a flood in 1936. From the bridge, you may hear the sound of nearby train horns. Following the route to its southern endpoint will take you past farmland to the East Deerfield Yard, an active rail yard at the end of the trail. While travel within the rail yard is not permitted, the trail is close enough to see and smell the locomotives in action—an intriguing observation point for railroad buffs.

Retracing your path will return you to Unity Park, where nearby restaurants and shops offer numerous opportunities for local cuisine and wares. Near the Unity Park parking lot, a large, well-designed playground—featuring wheelchair-accessible equipment—presents a great stopping point for families after enjoying the trail. The Fishway Visitor and Education Center (no admission fee) is also nearby, located behind Unity Park at First and Maple Streets in Turners Falls. If that puts you in the mood for fishing, you can do that at Unity Park too.

While the suggested starting point is Unity Park in Montague, trail parking is also provided near the rail yard in Deerfield. The trail may be accessed at either point.

CONTACT: **mass.gov/locations/canalside-rail-trail**

DIRECTIONS

To reach the Unity Park endpoint in Montague from I-91, take Exit 27 for MA 2 E toward Boston. Continue on MA 2 E for 2.5 miles, then turn right onto Main Road/Ave. A. Go 0.3 mile, then turn left onto First St. Unity Park will be on your right in 0.3 mile. Parking is located in several places, just past Montague Town Hall or at the ball fields a little farther down First St. The paved trailhead is located to the left of the parking lot behind the town hall.

To reach the southern endpoint in Deerfield from I-91, take Exit 26 for MA 2 W/MA 2A E toward Greenfield Center/North Adams. At the traffic circle, exit onto MA 2A E (the third exit if coming from the north, or the first exit if coming from the south). Go 0.6 mile, and turn right onto River St. Go 0.5 mile, continuing onto Mill St. In 0.3 mile, turn right onto Bank Row/Deerfield St. Go 1.1 miles, continuing onto Greenfield Road 0.2 mile. Turn left onto E. Deerfield Road/River Road, and go 0.9 mile. Turn left onto McClelland Farm Road. Parking at Railroad Yard Road, and the southern trailhead, will be on the left in 0.2 mile.

To reach the southern endpoint in Deerfield from US 5/MA 10, in Greenfield turn left onto River Road (at the Deerfield River) if coming from the north, or right if coming from the south. Go 0.9 mile. Turn left onto McClelland Farm Road. Parking at Railroad Yard Road, and the southern trailhead, will be on the left in 0.2 mile.

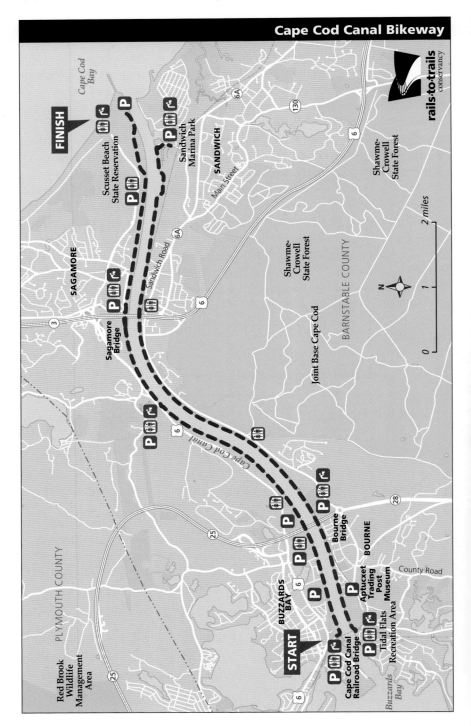

Though the idea for a Cape Cod Canal goes back to the settlers of Plymouth Colony, the waterway didn't begin construction until 1909. The U.S. Army Corps of Engineers took over operation and maintenance of the canal in 1928. Originally dirt roads on either side of the canal, paved service roads now double as the Cape Cod Canal Bikeway. Although there is no easy off-road route to cross the canal, each side of the bikeway offers a unique experience for trail users.

Starting from the visitor center in Buzzards Bay on the north side of the canal, the trail passes by recreational areas, including access to a short stone-surface trail in an open space nature preserve. In 0.6 mile this figure eight trail also features playground equipment, including a zip line and parcourse. Located just before and just after the Bourne Bridge, 1.3 miles into the trail, are RV camps with grills and recreational areas.

County
Barnstable

Endpoints
Visitor Center at Main St. between Academy Dr. and Off Cohasset Ave. (Buzzards Bay) to Scusset Beach State Reservation on Scusset Beach Road, 0.7 mile east of Williston Road (Sagamore Beach); and Tidal Flats Recreation Area at Canal Service Road, 0.1 mile north of Bell Road (Bourne), to Sandwich Marina Park at Freezer Road, 0.2 mile north of Ed Moffitt Dr. (Sandwich)

Mileage
13.9

Type
Canal/Rail-with-Trail

Roughness Index
1

Surface
Asphalt

The US 6 bridge makes for an interesting sight as you approach the trail's east end in Sagamore.

On the west end of the trail, you'll see the Cape Cod Canal Railroad Bridge.

The trail offers scenic views of the canal and chances to watch native birds scouting for fish or spot rabbits hopping across the trail. After passing under the Sagamore Bridge, 4.7 miles into the trail, you will soon reach the northern trailhead at the Scusset Beach State Reservation (7.1 miles from the visitor center). Sand dunes and grasses waving in the breeze mark the way to the picnic area, swimming beach, and rocky peninsula for walking at the end of the trail. Starting from the Tidal Flats Recreation Area in Bourne on the south side, head north through a parking lot and pass the Cape Cod Canal Railroad Bridge on your left. Interpretive signage shares the story and purpose of the railroad bridge. Not much farther along (0.6 mile into the trail) is trailside access to the Aptucxet Trading Post Museum. Settlers founded the trading post in 1627 to trade with American Indians and the Dutch for essential goods such as salt, sugar, and furs to pay off the debt incurred to reach Massachusetts.

Past the museum, canalside residential houses offer local charm on the right, while open views of the canal and Bourne Bridge (1.5 miles into the trail) dominate to the left. After the bridge, the trail leaves the residential neighborhoods behind and becomes abundant with trees and wildlife. Perhaps the most distinctive feature of the path is its use as an access point for recreational fishing along the shore of the canal. Many bicyclists even have fishing pole carriers on their bicycles.

After passing under the Sagamore Bridge 4.7 miles into the trail, the trail parallels the Cape Cod Central Railroad; you can see the ties of the rail line to your right. Nearing the end of the trail (6.4 miles from the Tidal Flats Recreation Area in Bourne) is an industrial area with a power plant and pipelines on the right and industrial docks on the left. Not long after, you will reach Sandwich Marina Park, where the trail ends at 6.7 miles. Here, the U.S. Army Corps of

Engineers maintains the Cape Cod Canal Visitor Center, where you can learn more about the history and natural area. The sprawling marina offers multiple dining options—perfect after a trail ride—and is a close bike ride into town if you want to explore Sandwich further.

Although the Tidal Flats Recreation Area in Bourne represents the south side of the trail, Friends of the Bourne Rail Trail—and Friends of Falmouth Bikeways—hope one day to extend the trail south to connect to the northern end of the Shining Sea Bikeway in Falmouth (see page 161). In addition, the East Coast Greenway may incorporate the Cape Cod Canal Bikeway into a new coastal route linking Boston and Providence, Rhode Island, via Cape Cod.

Other trails near Cape Cod Bay include the Province Lands Bike Trail (see page 153), Old Colony Nature Pathway, Old Colony Rail Trail (see page 146), Bridle Trail, and Hanover Branch Rail Trail.

CONTACTS: **www.nae.usace.army.mil/Missions/Recreation/Cape-Cod-Canal** and **capecodbikeguide.com/canal.asp**

DIRECTIONS

North of the canal: To reach the Scusset Beach State Reservation trailhead, take I-495 or I-195 to MA 25 S. From MA 25 (Blue Star Memorial Hwy.), take Exit 3 for US 6 toward Bourne/Hyannis. Go 0.5 mile to a traffic circle, then exit left to US 6 E/Main St. In 3.8 miles, merge onto Meetinghouse Lane, which becomes Scusset Beach Road in 0.4 mile. Follow Scusset Beach Road 0.8 mile to its end, where you'll find parking at the East Canal Lot to your right. Note that there is a daily fee for parking. For more information, visit **mass.gov/locations /scusset-beach-state-reservation.**

To reach the Buzzards Bay trailhead, take I-495 or I-195 to MA 25 S. From MA 25 (Blue Star Memorial Hwy.), take Exit 3 for US 6 toward Bourne/Hyannis. Go 0.5 mile to a traffic circle, then take the second exit onto US 6 W toward Buzzards Bay Bypass. Continue a little over 1 mile to the Buzzards Bay Rotary. At the rotary, take the third exit onto Main St. Go 0.3 mile, then turn right into the Visitor Center for parking. If you pass Wallace Ave. on your left, you've gone too far.

South of the canal: To reach the Tidal Flats Recreation Area trailhead, take I-495 or I-195 to MA 25 S. Take MA 25 S (Blue Star Memorial Hwy.) until it becomes MA 28 (10 miles past I-495). Go 0.8 mile, crossing the Bourne Bridge. At Bourne Rotary S., take the second exit onto Trowbridge Road, which becomes Shore Road in 0.7 mile. Continue another 0.6 mile, then turn right onto Bell Road. Continue straight 0.2 mile to two parking lots.

To reach the Sandwich Marina Park trailhead from US 6, take Exit 2 and head north on MA 130/Water St. In 1.4 miles, turn right onto Tupper Road, heading northwest toward Cape Cod Canal. Continue on Tupper Road 0.8 mile, then turn right onto Freezer Road. Follow Freezer Road 0.3 mile. Do not turn right into the private marina area; instead, continue straight to reach the playground area with public parking.

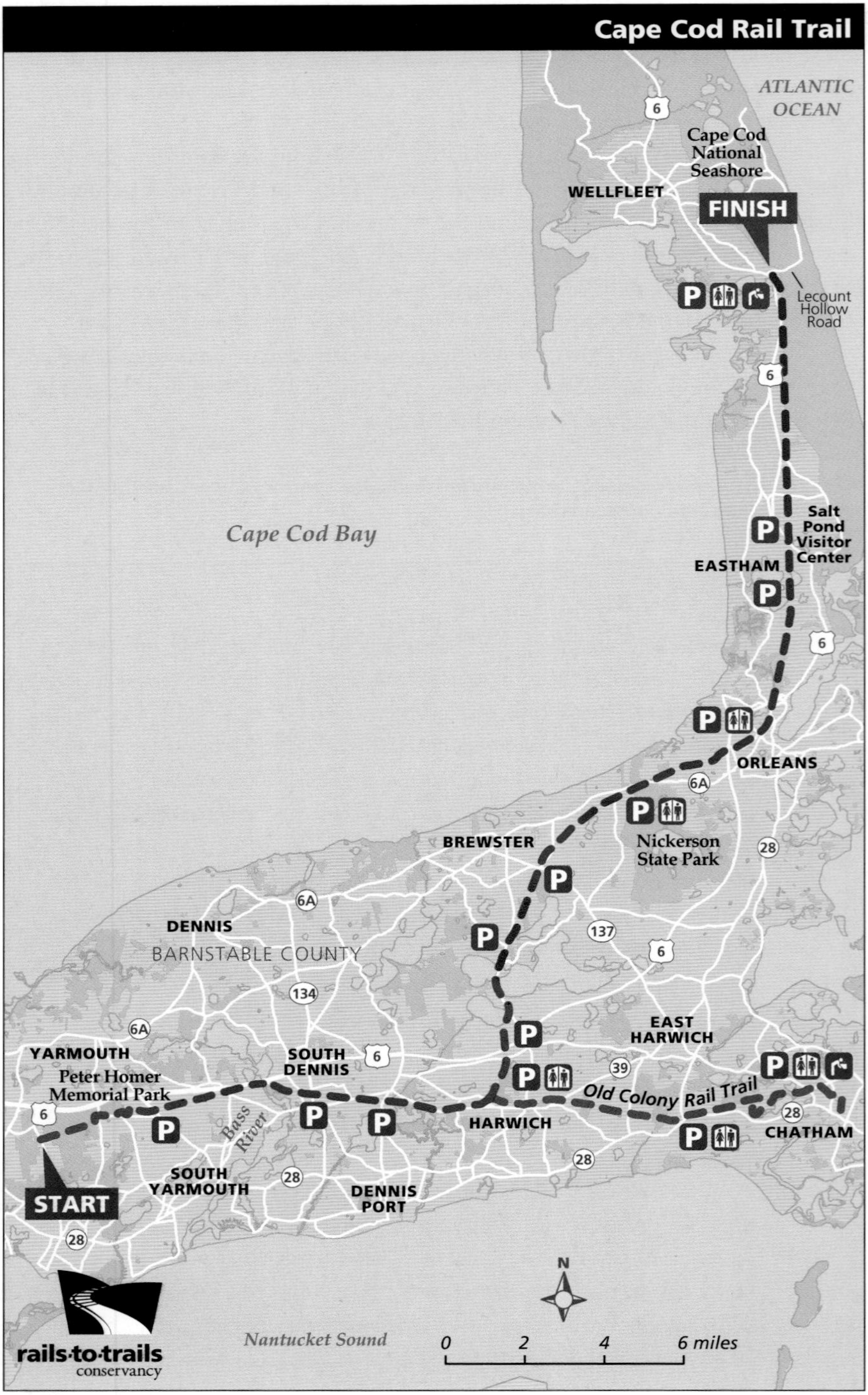
Cape Cod Rail Trail
ATLANTIC OCEAN
Cape Cod National Seashore
WELLFLEET
FINISH
Lecount Hollow Road
Cape Cod Bay
Salt Pond Visitor Center
EASTHAM
ORLEANS
BREWSTER
Nickerson State Park
DENNIS
BARNSTABLE COUNTY
EAST HARWICH
YARMOUTH
Peter Homer Memorial Park
SOUTH DENNIS
Old Colony Rail Trail
Bass River
HARWICH
CHATHAM
SOUTH YARMOUTH
DENNIS PORT
START
N
Nantucket Sound
0 2 4 6 miles
rails·to·trails conservancy

Cape Cod's briny seaports, sandy beaches, delectable seafood, and diverse landscape of salt marshes, pine forests, and cranberry bogs can all be experienced from the 27.5-mile Cape Cod Rail Trail. Completely paved and mostly flat, the trail is a popular destination for families and recreational bicyclists.

The route follows 19th-century rail lines that carried vacationers to the once remote peninsula from Boston and New York City. Between Yarmouth and Orleans, the trail follows the Cape Cod Central Railroad, completed in 1865. The Old Colony Railroad bought the line in 1872, then extended it from Orleans to Provincetown, past the trail's current endpoint in Wellfleet. Passenger service ceased in 1937, and freight hung on until the mid-1960s. By 1978 the trail was in place, and vacationers once again hit the corridor, but this time on foot, in-line skates, and bicycles.

The rail-trail starts at a long-awaited extension opened in 2017 in Yarmouth, where it meets a local bike trail at Peter Homer Memorial Park. (Long-range plans

While its sandy beaches garner much of the attention, the rail-trail's tranquil and wooded areas are no less worthy of exploration.

County
Barnstable

Endpoints
Yarmouth Trail in Peter Homer Memorial Park at 144 Old Town House Road (Yarmouth) to Lecount Hollow Road between Kincaid St. and US 6 (Wellfleet)

Mileage
27.5

Type
Rail-Trail

Roughness Index
1

Surface
Asphalt

call for extending the trail westward to Barnstable.) Crossing Station Avenue on a pedestrian bridge, the trail rolls through woods for 2.5 miles to a 160-foot bridge over the Bass River (scheduled for opening in late 2018; signs will be posted at the trailhead regarding the bridge status), and then another pedestrian bridge over MA 134 to an old trailhead in South Dennis.

The next 3 miles offer ample opportunities to picnic, indulge in ice cream, or detour to other trails and towns. The Cape Cod Rail Trail meets the Old Colony Rail Trail (see page 146) at a landscaped bicycle rotary with a picnic area and information kiosks in Harwich. That alternative trail heads east 7 miles through the Hacker Wildlife Sanctuary and ends in Chatham.

Heading north from the rotary on the Cape Cod Rail Trail, you'll soon be sailing past kettle ponds formed when glaciers melted, leaving behind pockets of freshwater enjoyed as swimming holes today. Quaint general stores provide refreshments that can be consumed on-site or at trailside picnic tables. Near mile 14 you'll reach Nickerson State Park, which offers swimming pools, picnic areas, walking and biking trails, restrooms, and camping throughout its 1,900 acres. The 8-mile forested trail here makes for a shady, cool ride.

The path joins a small road for a short distance 1.5 miles past Nickerson, crosses a bridge, and enters the bustling tourist town of Orleans. Boasting a variety of restaurants and specialty stores, this former whaling seaport is a good place to stop for lunch, shop, or visit historical sites. About 3.5 miles past Orleans you'll see signs to the Cape Cod National Seashore's Salt Pond Visitor Center, located about 0.5 mile off the trail.

The remaining miles offer public campgrounds and coastal overlooks. At trail's end, Wellfleet occupies a narrow strip of the cape, flanked by the Atlantic Ocean and Cape Cod Bay. A mile trip east on Lecount Hollow Road from the trailhead is rewarded with large dunes and a sandy ocean beach. Locally grown oysters are available in many restaurants and honored in October's Wellfleet Oyster Fest.

CONTACT: mass.gov/eea/agencies/dcr/massparks/region-south/cape-cod-rail-trail.html

DIRECTIONS

To reach the Yarmouth trailhead from US 6/Mid-Cape Hwy., take Exit 8 toward Yarmouth and head south on Station Ave. Go 0.5 mile and look for the trailhead parking on the left. To reach the end of the trail at Peter Homer Memorial Park, cross the pedestrian bridge and proceed west 0.4 mile.

To reach the Wellfleet trailhead from US 6, turn right onto Lecount Hollow Road/ Maguire Landing about 10 miles past Orleans. Go about 500 feet and look for trailhead parking on the right.

The Charles River Bike Path, also referred to as the Charles River Greenway, provides a paved, nearly 23-mile route from Boston to its western suburbs. The trail is also part of a larger, developing network called the East Coast Greenway, which stretches from Maine to Florida.

A large section of the trail, beginning on its eastern end and extending 16 miles, is named after Dr. Paul Dudley White, a prominent cardiologist and proponent of preventive medicine such as exercise. The Dr. Paul Dudley White Bike Path hugs each side of the Charles River through Boston, Cambridge, and Watertown.

In many sections of the route, multiple parallel trails present options for those who prefer an unpaved surface or would like to stay farther from the road activity. A number of architecturally interesting bridges will greet you as you enter Cambridge from Boston, allowing you to create shorter routes on both sides of the river as opposed to the

Skyline views, from Boston to its western suburbs, can be found on this trail.

Counties
Suffolk, Middlesex

Endpoints
Museum of Science at Charles River Dam Road, between Museum Way and Nashua St. (Boston), to Prospect St., 0.1 mile northwest of Crescent St. (Waltham)

Mileage
22.9

Type
Greenway/Non-Rail-Trail

Roughness Index
1

Surface
Asphalt

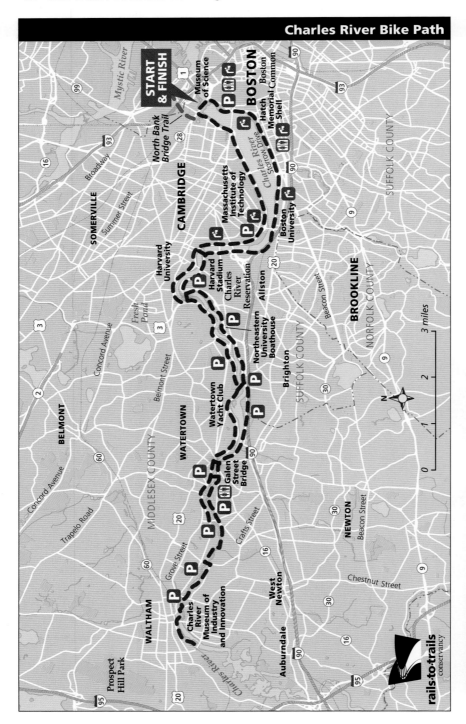

Charles River Bike Path

larger loop. While busy roads parallel the trail on both sides of the river, most of the route has trees and green space. Along the way, you can enjoy watching boats skim by and even try your hand at a variety of water sports that are available to the public at numerous locations.

Starting at the famed Museum of Science in Boston and heading into Cambridge, the Charles River will be on your left for the first half of the loop. In 2 miles, Massachusetts Institute of Technology's campus will greet you on the right, followed by Harvard University in 2.6 miles. Continuing another 3.8 miles into Watertown, you'll pass the Watertown Yacht Club to your left as you curve around the river, followed by the Pat and Gabriel Farren Playground on your right, just before Irving Street.

If you'd like to extend your ride farther at this point, you can continue on the Charles River Bike Path beyond Watertown west to Waltham. This option provides the opportunity to visit Waltham's Charles River Museum of Industry and Innovation.

Otherwise, cross the Galen Street Bridge to begin the other side of the loop back to Boston. A number of athletic facilities, as well as the Northeastern University Boathouse, feature impressive modern architecture as you head east. Keep an eye out for rowers carrying their boats across the trail. In 2.9 miles from the Galen Street Bridge, you'll come to the Charles River Reservation. This 20-mile stretch provides a quiet and natural experience with a dock, allowing you to enjoy an intimate view of the river as you curve around Soldiers Field Road, passing Harvard Stadium and Soldiers Field Park Children's Center on your right.

As you approach Boston, beautiful views of the city skyline will become visible. The trail traffic will also increase markedly, so stay vigilant. Soon, you'll pass bridges at Western Avenue and River Street, followed by the Boston University Bridge, with views of Boston University on your right. In 2.3 miles from Boston University Bridge, you'll come to an enchanting esplanade where the land extends into the water, connecting to the mainland through a series of quaint footbridges. There, you can take a break to catch a performance at the Hatch Memorial Shell, an outdoor concert venue. If nothing is scheduled, you can still marvel at its impressive design while enjoying a snack from the nearby concession stand.

Follow the trail for another 0.9 mile to its endpoint at the Museum of Science. If you'd like to extend your trip at this endpoint, head northeast from the museum for one block to the 0.5-mile North Bank Bridge trail. It begins at Museum Way and Education Street, traverses Cambridge's North Point Park, and ends in Paul Revere Park, Charlestown.

CONTACT: mass.gov/locations/charles-river-reservation

DIRECTIONS

To reach the Boston endpoint at the Museum of Science from I-93, take Exit 26 toward Storrow Dr. Go 0.5 mile and use the left lane to follow signs for MA 28 N/Leverett Circle/N. Station. Keep left to continue on Nashua St. toward MA 28 N/Charles River Dam Road. Continue on MA 28 N/Charles River Dam Road 0.3 mile, then turn left onto Museum of Science Driveway. Use the Museum of Science parking garage. Note that this is a paid garage. For more information, visit **mos.org/parking.**

If starting in Boston, consider using public transportation to avoid Boston's heavy traffic. The Science Park/West End Green Line Station of the MBTA subway, or T, deposits passengers steps away from the trail and the Museum of Science. Note that bikes (except folding bikes) are not permitted on the Green Line. However, the Orange Line welcomes bikes except 7–10 a.m. and 4–7 p.m. on weekdays. Use the Orange Line's Haymarket Station. Upon exiting Haymarket Station, turn right onto Congress St. toward Haymarket Square. In 0.2 mile, continue onto Merrimac St., then turn right onto Causeway St. in 0.1 mile. Take an immediate left onto Lomasney Way, then veer right to continue onto Nashua St. in 0.1 mile. Go 0.4 mile, then turn right onto Charles River Dam Road. The Museum of Science will be on your left.

To reach parking in Watertown from I-90 E/Massachusetts Turnpike, take Exit 17 toward Newton/Watertown. In 0.3 mile, turn right onto Centre St., following signs for Watertown. Make an immediate right onto Jefferson St. In 0.2 mile, turn right onto Maple St., making another immediate right onto Nonantum Road. In 0.9 mile, continue onto N. Beacon St. In 0.2 mile, use the left lane to enter the traffic circle. Follow it all the way through until you're heading west on Nonantum Road. Continue on Nonantum Road 0.5 mile. The Newton Yacht Club will be to your right. You will cross the trail to enter the parking lot, which is 1 mile from the Watertown endpoint on the southern bank of the Charles River. From I-90 W, take Exit 17 and merge onto Washington St. In 0.2 mile turn left to cross over I-90 and merge onto Centre St. In 0.1 mile turn right onto Maple St., and follow the directions above from there.

In Waltham, parking is available on the south bank of the Charles River, opposite the Charles River Museum of Industry & Innovation. From I-95, take Exit 26 for US 20 E to Waltham. Head east on US 20 for 1.9 miles as it becomes Weston St. and later Main St. Take a right onto Moody St. Take Moody 0.3 mile as you cross the Charles River. Take a left onto Pine St. In one block take a left onto Cooper St. and look for the large parking lot on your left.

The Clipper City Rail Trail is part of the Coastal Trails Coalition, which is developing in the four towns of Amesbury, Newbury, Newburyport, and Salisbury along the Merrimack River and will eventually be a link in the 28-mile Border to Boston Trail (see page 72).

While delivering wonderful views of the Merrimack River, the trail is set apart by its trailside art. More than a dozen sculptures, ranging from figurative to abstract to interactive art for children and families, are installed along the Clipper City Rail Trail. The sculptures serve as visual focal points that enhance this unique public space and draw people along the trail. The murals, custom planters, garden installations, custom signage, boardwalk, pedestrian bridge, and other functional elements are all designed with a special touch.

When complete, the Clipper City Rail Trail will be a full loop. At present, 3.9 miles of the loop are complete,

More than a dozen sculptures adorn the path.

County
Essex

Endpoints
MBTA Newburyport Station at US 1 and Parker St. to Parker St. between Hines Way and Oak Hill Cemetery (Newburyport)

Mileage
3.9

Type
Rail-Trail

Roughness Index
1

Surfaces
Asphalt, Boardwalk

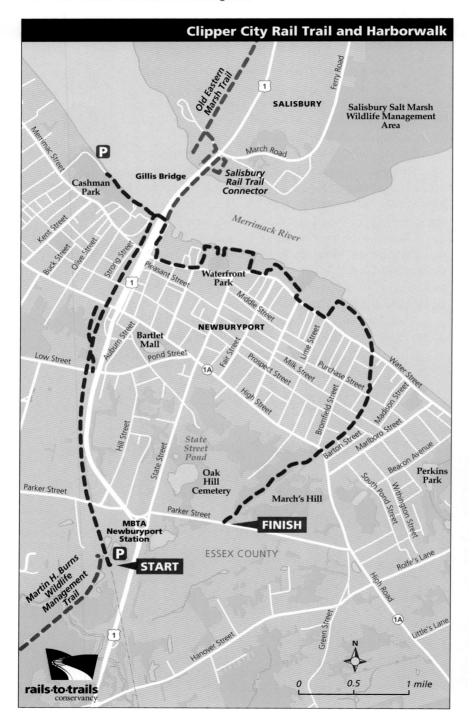

Clipper City Rail Trail and Harborwalk

SALISBURY

Salisbury Salt Marsh
Wildlife Management
Area

Old Eastern Marsh Trail

Ferry Road

March Road

Merrimac Street

Gillis Bridge

Cashman
Park

Salisbury
Rail Trail
Connector

Merrimack River

Kent Street

Buck Street

Olive Street

Strong Street

Pleasant Street

Waterfront
Park

Middle Street

Low Street

Auburn Street

Bartlet
Mall

Pond Street

NEWBURYPORT

Fair Street

Prospect Street

Milk Street

Lime Street

Purchase Street

Water Street

Madison Street

High Street

Bromfield Street

Barton Street

Marlboro Street

Hill Street

State Street

State
Street
Pond

Oak
Hill
Cemetery

March's Hill

South Pond Street

Withington Street

Beacon Avenue

Perkins
Park

Parker Street

Parker Street

MBTA
Newburyport
Station

FINISH

START

ESSEX COUNTY

Rolfe's Lane

Martin H. Burns
Wildlife
Management
Trail

Hanover Street

Green Street

High Road

Little's Lane

N

rails·to·trails
conservancy

0   0.5   1 mile

starting at the Massachusetts Bay Transportation Authority (MBTA) Newburyport Station and ending at Parker Street at the base of the Oak Hill Cemetery. If you are a confident road cyclist, however, you can travel the last 0.5 mile on-road to complete the loop.

There is no parking at the Parker Street endpoint adjacent to Oak Hill Cemetery, so it is recommended that you either start at Newburyport Station or from the center of Newburyport, as you are only six blocks from the trail in either direction. (Note that the Newburyport Station parking lot charges a daily fee.)

If arriving by MBTA train, your adventure starts immediately upon debarking because the route starts at the station platform. On the other side of Newburyport Station is the trailhead for the 3.4-mile trail within the Martin Burns Wildlife Management Area. This rail-trail, while more isolated and primitive, is an enjoyable experience nonetheless.

Once you descend the platform's northern ramp, you immediately will see large and unique outdoor sculptures along its wider greenway. The compelling use of wood, steel, and glass captures the flora, fauna, and heritage of the river corridor. *Steam Loco*, a play locomotive train, is a particular favorite for children and families. In 1.5 miles, you'll come to the Merrimack River, where you can enjoy a wonderful view of the active shoreline and Gillis Bridge, which takes US 1 over the river.

If you would like to add a diversion and cross the river, the 0.3-mile paved Salisbury Rail Trail Connector will take you safely under US 1 to the north bank of the Merrimack River, providing panoramic views of the harbor, marinas, and Newburyport riverfront. If biking, make sure to walk your bike on the bridge sidewalk. Immediately across the river, you will hit the 1.4-mile paved Old Eastern Marsh Trail, which features excellent interpretation and bird-watching.

If you aren't taking the side excursion, you can turn left once you reach Merrimack River to reach Cashman Park in less than 0.5 mile. The park offers tennis and basketball courts, a playground, a boat ramp, and other amenities. Otherwise, head east from the Gillis Bridge and continue along the Merrimack River; the portion of the trail along the river is known as the Harborwalk.

After passing through some boatyards, you'll come to Waterfront Park. If biking, make sure to walk your bike along the boardwalk promenade until the asphalt continues. You are now in the recently completed Phase II of the Clipper City Rail Trail project. Throughout this section of construction, planners and designers continued using superior materials and innovative solutions, including the High Street underpass. After this short tunnel, the next 0.5 mile is set in a very different landscape—wooded and serene. The trail ends at Parker Street. Take care on this road and the traffic circle if you choose to head back to Newburyport Station to complete the loop.

CONTACT: cityofnewburyport.com/planning-development/pages/clipper-city -rail-trail-and-harborwalk

DIRECTIONS

Parking is available at Cashman Park (5 Pop Crowley Way) along the waterfront. To reach it from I-95, take Exit 57 for MA 113. Head northeast on MA 113 E/Storey Ave. Stay on MA 113 for 1.7 miles to a left turn on Broad St. Continue on Broad St. 0.3 mile to a right turn on Merrimac St., followed by an immediate left, which will take you directly into the park's parking lot.

Paid MBTA parking lots are located off of Parker St. at the head of the trail. To reach the MBTA Newburyport Station endpoint, take I-95 to Exit 56, and head east on Scotland Road. In 2 miles continue onto Parker St., and go another 0.6 mile. Turn right to stay on Parker St., and go 0.4 mile. Turn right onto US 1 and follow signs 0.1 mile to the MBTA station. Once at the station, go up onto the main station's ramp and platform and follow it to the end, where it becomes the trail.

There is no parking available at the trailhead near Hines Way.

The 2.4-mile Columbia Greenway Rail Trail and the 6.5-mile Southwick Rail Trail together form a seamless, paved route in rural south-central Massachusetts.

Start at the northern end on Westfield's Main Street, which has ample parking and numerous nearby businesses. Heading south, the Columbia Greenway Rail Trail has an open feel, and its separated grade crossings allow you to keep rolling or walking. Adjacent neighborhoods connect to the trail via direct access points. Along the way, you will pass by tobacco and other farms and cross the Little River as you make your way toward the northern starting point of the Southwick Rail Trail.

You might not even notice the transition from one trail to the other as you cross Shaker Road. The Southwick

The Southwick Rail Trail provides a combination of canopied and sun-dappled stretches through rural south-central Massachusetts.

County
Hampden

Endpoints
Main St./US 20 between Free St. and Mechanic St. (Westfield) to the MA–CT state line 0.8 mile south of the intersection of Miller Road and Fourth St. (Southwick)

Mileage
8.9

Type
Rail-Trail

Roughness Index
1

Surface
Asphalt

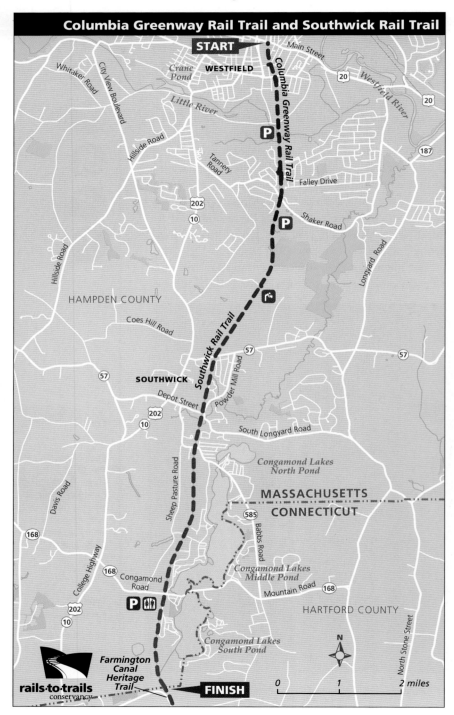

Columbia Greenway Rail Trail and Southwick Rail Trail

START

Main Street

Whitaker Road

City View Boulevard

Crane Pond   WESTFIELD

20

Westfield River

20

Little River

P

187

Hillside Road

Tannery Road

Falley Drive

202
10

P

Shaker Road

Longyard Road

Hillside Road

HAMPDEN COUNTY

Coes Hill Road

Columbia Greenway Rail Trail

Southwick Rail Trail

57

57

57

SOUTHWICK

Depot Street

Powder Mill Road

202
10

South Longyard Road

Congamond Lakes North Pond

MASSACHUSETTS

CONNECTICUT

Sheep Pasture Road

585

Babbs Road

168

Davis Road

College Highway

168

Congamond Road

Congamond Lakes Middle Pond

Mountain Road   168

HARTFORD COUNTY

202
10

P

North Stone Street

Congamond Lakes South Pond

N

rails·to·trails
conservancy

Farmington Canal Heritage Trail

FINISH

0   1   2 miles

Rail Trail offers a peaceful setting of farmland and open space that provides a combination of canopied and sunlight stretches. Along the way, you'll find numerous rest stops and occasional hiking paths leading into the adjoining forestlands. Conveniently located at the Congamond Road crossing, a couple of businesses are housed in buildings that once served as a station for the New Haven and Northampton Railroad.

As you reach the trail's southern end, you will encounter the Massachusetts–Connecticut state line. From here, another pathway called the Farmington Canal Heritage Trail (see page 19) continues more than 40 miles farther south to New Haven, Connecticut. If you decide to continue riding, know that the trail has varied surfaces, as well as some gaps in the route, so it's best to plan ahead.

CONTACT: columbiagreenway.org and **southwickrailtrail.org**

DIRECTIONS

Columbia Greenway Rail Trail: The northern parking area in Westfield is on Main St., just east of Broad St. From I-90, take Exit 3 for US 202. Head south on US 202/N. Elm St. for 1.7 miles. Make a U-turn around Park Square to head north on Broad St., and turn right onto Main St. In one block the trail will be on your right.

Southwick Rail Trail: To reach the trail's northern endpoint from I-90, take Exit 3, and head south on US 202/N. Elm St. In 1.8 miles turn right onto Court St., go 0.1 mile, and turn left onto Pleasant St., which becomes S. Maple St. and then Southwick Road. Go a total of 2 miles, and turn left onto Tannery Road. Turn left onto Ponders Hollow Road/Shaker Road, and go 0.9 mile to Shaker Farms Country Club. From the intersection of MA 168 and US 202 in Southwick, head north on US 202 for 3.7 miles and turn right onto Tannery Road. Travel 1.9 miles and take a right onto Ponders Hollow Road/Shaker Road. Continue 0.9 mile to the entrance of the Shaker Farms Country Club (866 Shaker Road, Westfield). Follow the entrance road through the club's main parking lot to the smaller trailhead parking lot adjacent to the trail.

To reach the trail's southern endpoint from I-90, take Exit 3, and head south on US 202/N. Elm St. In 1.8 miles turn right onto Court St., go 0.1 mile, and turn left onto Pleasant St., which becomes S. Maple St. and then Southwick Road. Go a total of 9.8 miles, entering Connecticut, and turn left onto Notch Road. Take an immediate left onto Quarry Road. Travel 1.7 miles and turn left onto Phelps Road. Look for the trail's parking lot on the right side of Phelps Road.

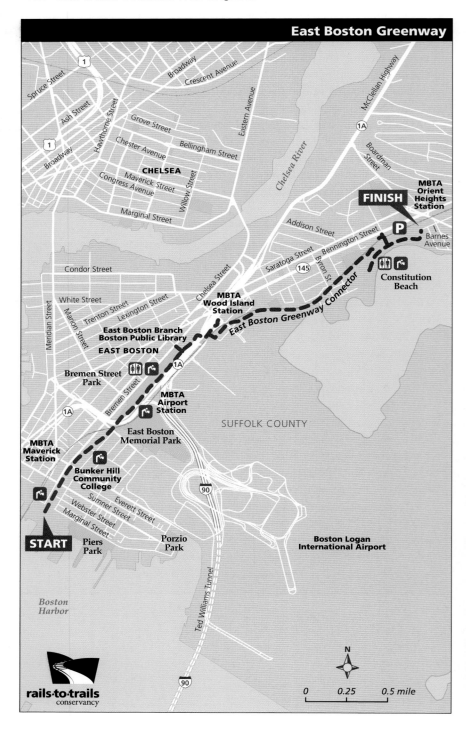

East Boston Greenway

More and more, airport lands near previously under-used rail corridors are being transformed from largely neglected vacant lands into urban greenways. These new vibrant spaces are used not only by residents but also by those who would rather start their bicycle vacation from a major airport. The East Boston Greenway is a perfect example of this new dynamic.

If you have a long layover at Boston Logan International Airport, this nearby trail is a good way to reenergize yourself. Alternatively, the airport's service road from the terminal is also open to bicyclists. The Massachusetts Port Authority (Massport) operates this rail-with-trail along active tracks and has linked several green spaces that now total almost 15 acres. The heavily used corridor sections are gated and closed in the evening, but usually not until 8 p.m. in the summer. The parks within the longer corridor stay open later and are heavily used by families from adjacent neighborhoods. The parks include playgrounds, spray parks, and bike rentals.

Much of the rail-with-trail parallels the MBTA commuter line.

County
Suffolk

Endpoints
Marginal St. and Orleans St. to Constitution Beach at Barnes Ave. west of Thurston St. (Boston)

Mileage
2.8

Type
Greenway/Rail-with-Trail

Roughness Index
1

Surfaces
Asphalt, Sand

Beginning at the southern trailhead on Marginal Street, take in the views from the Boston skyline, just across the harbor. Heading north (the trail has separate, parallel bicycle and pedestrian tracks), the East Boston Greenway will take you under Sumner Street, where a satellite campus of Bunker Hill Community College is located on your right. You'll pass a number of commercial and residential properties as you pass under Maverick and Porter Streets. Five miles from the trailhead, you'll pass under the East Boston Expressway, followed by Bremen Street Park and the East Boston Branch of the Boston Public Library on your left.

After crossing back under the East Boston Expressway, the East Boston Greenway turns into the 0.5-mile, newly developed East Boston Greenway Connector, which takes you along an active railroad that runs through the heart of the East Boston Greenway. The rail's art and design, including a restored caboose, reflect the area's industrial heritage. You'll pass the Massachusetts Bay Transportation Authority (MBTA) Wood Island Station to your left and Boston Logan International Airport, followed by views of Boston's waterfront, on your right. Follow the East Boston Greenway Connector until you reach the northern endpoint at Constitution Beach.

Constitution Beach includes a bathhouse, concessions, playgrounds, sports facilities, an ice rink, and ample parking. The beach is a perfect place to sit at night and watch the jets take off across the bay.

CONTACT: bostonplans.org/planning/planning-initiatives/east-boston-greenway

DIRECTIONS

The East Boston Greenway is most easily visited using the MBTA Blue Line subway and going to Maverick Station, near the south endpoint; Orient Heights Station, near the north endpoint; or Wood Island Station, located in the middle of the rail-trail. To reach the East Boston Greenway from Boston Logan International Airport, take the free Massport shuttle bus to the MBTA Airport Station, situated in the middle of the East Boston Greenway.

To reach the northern trailhead at Constitution Beach from I-90, take I-90 east until it becomes MA 1A N. Take the exit for MA 145/Bennington St. toward Winthrop/Chelsea, and travel north 0.1 mile. Continue onto Vienna St. for a few hundred feet, then take a slight right onto MA 145/Bennington St. Go 1 mile, then turn right onto Saratoga St. In a few hundred feet, turn right onto Bayswater St. Take the next right onto Barnes Ave., and follow it to the parking lot that runs the whole length of the beach.

The overall goal of the Grand Trunk Trail in south-central Massachusetts is to connect the communities of Brimfield, Sturbridge, and Southbridge by trail. Currently, two sections of the trail are completed. Although they do not yet connect, they are both pleasant rides through the Quinebaug River valley and worthy of tying together for a day of adventure and railroad history.

The Grand Trunk Trail is also part of an effort to create a larger 66-mile regional trail known as the Titanic Rail Trail that will run from Palmer to Franklin. The Titanic Rail Trail gets its name from the former president of the Grand Trunk Railway, Charles M. Hays, who lost his life sailing back from England on the RMS *Titanic* just after securing the necessary funds to complete a second transcontinental railroad. The venture was never completed.

The Brimfield Section offers an easy jaunt through wooded lands and cut-stone embankments.

Counties
Hampden, Worcester

Endpoints
US 20, 0.2 mile southeast of W. Old Sturbridge Road, to E. Brimfield Holland Road, 0.4 mile south of US 20 (Brimfield); and River Road, 0.5 mile north of Mashapaug Road (Sturbridge), to the Westville Dam at Marjorie Lane, 0.5 mile north of South St. (Southbridge)

Mileage
6.2

Type
Rail-Trail

Roughness Index
2

Surfaces
Crushed Stone, Dirt, Gravel

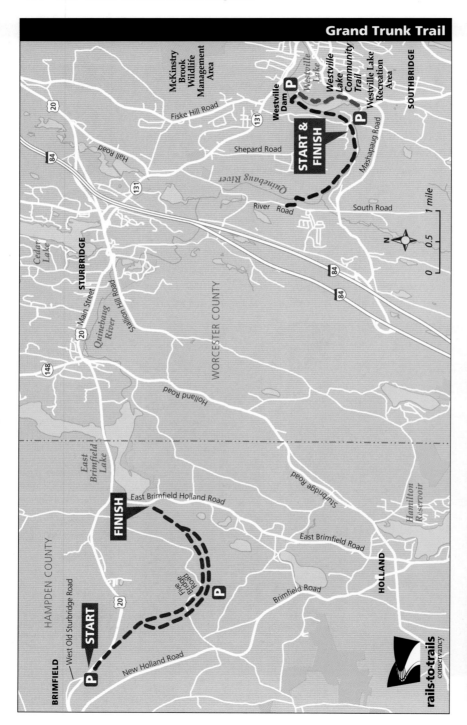

Brimfield Section

Depart from the western end of the trail on the outskirts of Brimfield and ride southeast for an easy jaunt through wooded lands and cut-stone embankments. You can quickly see how early railroads were competing for land and revenue opportunities.

For most of its route, the trail is actually comprised of two paralleling former railbeds, both usually within viewing sight of one another. One line was owned by the Southern New England Railway, a subsidiary of Grand Trunk Railway of Canada; the other tracks belonged to a trolley line that ran between Southbridge and Springfield. Although most of the trail is along the trolley alignment, this section of the larger gauge Grand Trunk Railway is the trail's namesake.

The trail effectively ends on the western bank of the Quinebaug River. Though you won't find a bridge over the river, another 0.5 mile of trail continues on the eastern bank and runs up to East Brimfield Holland Road.

Westville Lake Section

On the west end of Southbridge, you can enjoy a pleasant ride on the rail-trail and a loop around Westville Lake. The best place to begin your adventure is the

The Ed Calcutt Bridge crosses the Quinebaug River in the Westville Lake Section of the trail.

trailhead parking lot located at the Westville Lake Recreation Area. Heading northeast from here, you will be riding along a mostly tree-covered path dotted with picnic tables for welcome breaks.

The route takes you across the Westville Dam, which you may not really appreciate the size of until you are right up on it. The structure is 78 feet high and 560 feet across. From there, you can continue around the east side of the lake on the Westville Lake Community Trail, which will lead you back to the parking lot.

After the loop, you can continue southwest on the trail, where it will traverse forest and end just beyond the Quinebaug River crossing. The metal bridge across the river provides access to River Road.

CONTACT: www.nae.usace.army.mil/Missions/Recreation/WestfieldLake.aspx and **sturbridgetrails.org**

DIRECTIONS

Brimfield Section: From I-90 take Exit 8 to MA 32/US 20. Turn right (south) onto MA 32/Thorndike St., and go 0.7 mile. Turn left onto US 20/Park St., and go 9.3 miles. The parking lot will be on your right.

Or from downtown Brimfield, take US 20 E 1.2 miles to the Brimfield trailhead. You will see the parking lot on your right; look for the brown sign labeled GRAND TRUNK TRAIL BRIMFIELD SECTION.

Westville Lake Section: Take I-84 to Exit 2. If coming from the north, turn left onto Old Sturbridge Village Road, and almost immediately take another left onto River Road. If coming from the south, turn right onto River Road. In 1.6 miles turn left onto Mashapaug Road, and go 1.1 miles. Turn left onto Breakneck Road, and the trail parking lot will be on your right in 0.4 mile.

Or from downtown Southbridge, take Main St./MA 131 W out of town. When the road forks, veer left onto South St. Continue 1.1 miles until you see a road split off to your right; though unmarked, this is Off S St. Drive on this street 0.4 mile to a small bridge over the Quinebaug River, where the roadway becomes Breakneck Road. The parking lot will appear immediately on your right after the crossing.

The 5.3-mile Independence Greenway makes for a pleasant ride, providing access to lakes, parks, and nature preserves. The paved pathway is located in the town of Peabody (pronounced by locals as "pea-biddy"), which is known as the Leather City thanks to its historical tannery industry. Be on the lookout for a variety of bird species, as well as the occasional snake sunning itself on the trail's paved surface. For most of the ride, you will enjoy a natural setting; however, some neighboring homes are visible along the trail for a portion of the trip.

Starting at the northwestern trailhead on Russell Street, you'll follow the Ipswich River on your left, followed by the Norris Brook Wetlands. In 1.3 miles, be aware that the trail passes along an Aggregate Industries quarry, where blasting occurs on Thursdays at 1 p.m. during the summer. One horn means blasting will commence in

The east end of the greenway traverses the verdant Proctor Brook valley.

County
Essex

Endpoints
Russell St. between
Boston St. and Birch St.
to Essex Center Dr. near
Lahey Medical Center,
Peabody, across from
MA 128/Yankee Division
Hwy. (Peabody)

Mileage
5.3

Type
Rail-Trail

Roughness Index
1

Surface
Asphalt

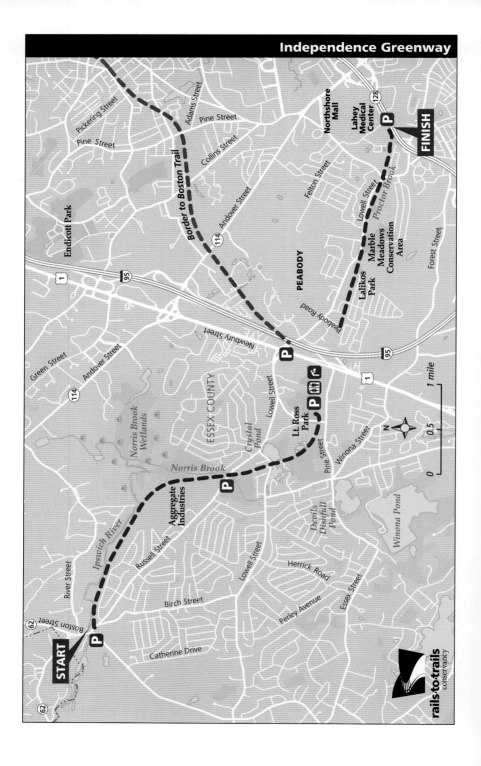

5 minutes. If you hear two horns, make sure to move away from the area, as blasting is in progress.

In 0.9 mile from the quarry, after passing another trailhead and parking area at Russell Street and Norris Brook, you'll pass the Crystal Pond trailhead on your left. In another 0.9 mile, the Lt. Ross Park trailhead, which includes a playground, baseball field, and soda machine, makes for a great break spot. Note that a gap of more than 1 mile exists between the Lt. Ross Park trailhead and the next trailhead at Peabody Road. This gap requires you to ride with traffic. Coming out of Lt. Ross Park, take a right onto Johnson Street, continuing onto Lowell Street in 0.5 mile, and turning right onto Peabody Road in just under 1 mile. Only experienced road riders should take this route; a sidewalk is available for walkers. This on-road route also connects to the Border to Boston Trail (see page 72).

At the Peabody Road trailhead, the path follows Proctor Brook, as well as Lalikos Park and Marble Meadows Conservation Area on the right. As you near the end of the trail, you will begin to hear the buzz of traffic. There are a number of road crossings as well. Cross carefully at the busy intersection of Prospect and Lowell Streets. The trail ends at the Northshore Mall trailhead. With the trailhead's namesake at the base of the trail, you can stop for a snack, bathroom break, or some retail therapy.

CONTACT: peabody-ma.gov/comm_dev/IndependenceGreenwayMap.pdf

DIRECTIONS

To reach the northwestern endpoint on Russell St. from I-95, take Exit 41 for Main St. toward Lynnfield Center/Wakefield. Turn right onto Main St., and go 3.6 miles. Continue on Boston St. 0.4 mile, then turn right onto Russell St. Parking will be on your right, with the trail endpoint located across the street from the lot, near the Ipswich River.

To reach the Northshore Mall trailhead from I-95, take Exit 45 to merge onto MA 128 N toward Gloucester. In about 2.6 miles, take Exit 25A toward Lowell St./W. Peabody. In 0.1 mile, continue right (west) onto Northshore Road. In another 0.1 mile, turn right onto Essex Center Dr., then take an immediate left to continue on Essex Center Dr. 0.2 mile. Parking and the trailhead will be on your right, just past the Lahey Medical Center.

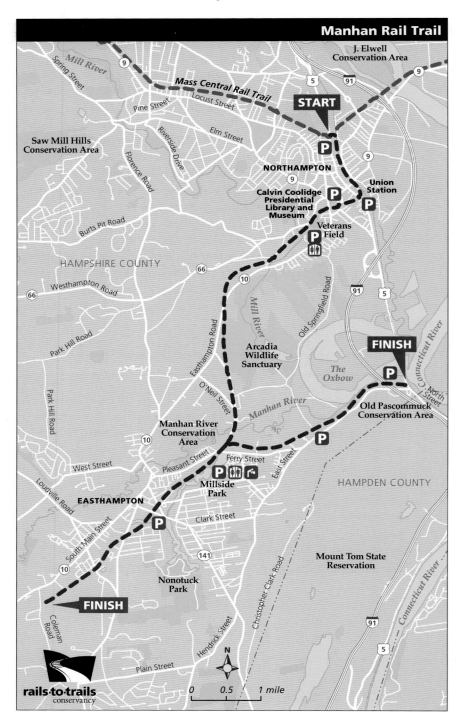

Manhan Rail Trail

J. Elwell Conservation Area

Mill River
Spring Street
Mass Central Rail Trail
Pine Street
Locust Street
Elm Street
Riverside Drive
Florence Road

Saw Mill Hills Conservation Area

START

NORTHAMPTON

Calvin Coolidge Presidential Library and Museum

Union Station

Veterans Field

Burts Pit Road

HAMPSHIRE COUNTY

Westhampton Road

Park Hill Road

Mill River

Old Springfield Road

Arcadia Wildlife Sanctuary

The Oxbow

FINISH

Connecticut River

North Street

Old Pascommuck Conservation Area

Easthampton Road

O'Neil Street

Manhan River

Manhan River Conservation Area

West Street

Pleasant Street

Ferry Street

East Street

Millside Park

HAMPDEN COUNTY

Loudville Road

EASTHAMPTON

Clark Street

Park Hill Road

South Main Street

Nonotuck Park

Mount Tom State Reservation

Christopher Clark Road

Connecticut River

FINISH

Coleman Road

Hendrick Street

Plain Street

N

0   0.5   1 mile

rails·to·trails
conservancy

The Manhan Rail Trail, well integrated into the local communities it serves, offers a pleasant ride or stroll. It conveniently weaves together parks, community points of interest, neighborhoods, and business centers.

Shaped like a Y tipped to its side, the northwest section—also known as the New Haven and Northampton Canal Line—leads into the charming city of Northampton, which is the seat of government for Hampshire County. At its northern end at King Street, the trail also connects to two sections of the Mass Central Rail Trail (see page 118), extending the mileage options for longer rides, jogs, and walks. Equestrians are permitted to use the Manhan Rail Trail too, so long as they clean up after their animals.

Heading southward from this point, the trail is adjacent to, but nicely separated from, an active railroad line and a fine example of a rail-with-trail facility that enhances connectivity. Union Station offers a new twist on an old

This colorful mural is located in Easthampton near a former train depot.

County
Hampshire

Endpoints
King St., just north of Church St., and North St./Mount Tom Road, just north of East St. (Northampton), to Coleman Road, just south of MA 10 (Easthampton)

Mileage
9.6

Type
Rail-Trail/Rail-with-Trail

Roughness Index
1

Surface
Asphalt

railroad building, and there are numerous restaurants, cafés, and shops to enjoy here after a good day of exploring the Pioneer Valley area. Farther southwest, you'll also find the Calvin Coolidge Presidential Library and Museum within close proximity of the trail.

Continuing south, you begin to leave the city, and the trail runs by Veterans Field. Parking and restroom facilities are located here, along with a skate park where local boarders and riders defy gravity while enjoying their own space to recreate. After crossing the trestle at Mill River, the path becomes more suburban and even has a rural feel.

When you reach the junction of the Y, you can either continue south on the Manhan Rail Trail into Easthampton or ride 2.2 miles northeast to where the trail ends at North Street. If you choose the latter, you will parallel the Manhan and Connecticut Rivers and have access to the Old Pascommuck Conservation Area; this leg ends shortly after passing underneath I-91.

Heading south at the junction into Easthampton, you will begin to encounter neighborhoods, trailside businesses, and community gardens where you will find the Little Free Library for a quick read. A wonderful mural is located across the trail from the former depot. It depicts the many faces and professions of the community and how railroad once served local commerce. The trail continues to the south for a little over a mile to where it ends at a small turnaround and rest stop at Coleman Road.

CONTACT: manhanrailtrail.org

DIRECTIONS

In Northampton, public parking is available in Veterans Field. It can be reached from nearby I-91 by taking Exit 18. Head north on US 5/Mount Tom Road. In 0.2 mile at the roundabout, take the second exit onto Conz St. In 0.5 mile turn left onto Old South St., then in 0.1 mile turn right onto South St. In 0.2 mile take a left onto Main St., then a quick left onto West St. Veterans Field will be on your left. Be aware of trail users as you cross the trail to reach the parking.

Parking in Easthampton can also be accessed from I-91 by taking Exit 18. Head south on US 5/Mount Tom Road toward Easthampton. Travel 1.3 miles and turn right onto East St. Continue on East St. 1.4 miles, then turn right onto Ferry St. Continue 0.9 mile to just before the Manhan Rail Trail crosses the road; turn left at the unmarked street, which leads to a parking lot in Millside Park.

The Marblehead Rail-Trail appears on maps as a Y resting on its side, connecting Marblehead and Salem in the north and the city limits of Swampscott in the west. The 4-mile trail knits together a coastal area that's steeped in Colonial history, from *The Spirit of '76* painting hanging in a Marblehead museum to the infamous Salem witch trials of the 1690s. The trail is also part of the East Coast Greenway, a developing 3,000-mile trail system stretching from Maine to Florida.

The rail-trail follows a short spur of the historical Eastern Railroad, which launched service from Boston to Salem in 1838 and eventually served the coastline from Boston to Portland, Maine. The Marblehead spur opened in 1839 to connect that fishing village to Salem on the main line, followed by another branch linking Marblehead to the Swampscott depot. The rival Boston & Maine Railroad bought the Eastern Railroad in 1890 and operated the Marblehead branch until 1959. In the 1970s the Massachusetts Bay Transportation Authority (MBTA) acquired the main line, where it runs commuter trains.

County
Essex

Endpoints
Bessom St. between Round House Road and Bowden St. (Marblehead) to Canal St. between Rose St. and Kimball Road (Salem); and to Seaview Ave. between Humphrey St. and Atlantic Ave./MA 129 (Marblehead)

Mileage
4.0

Type
Rail-Trail

Roughness Index
1–2

Surfaces
Asphalt, Dirt, Gravel, Sand

Hardwood forests, wetlands, and easy access to nature are part of this trail experience.

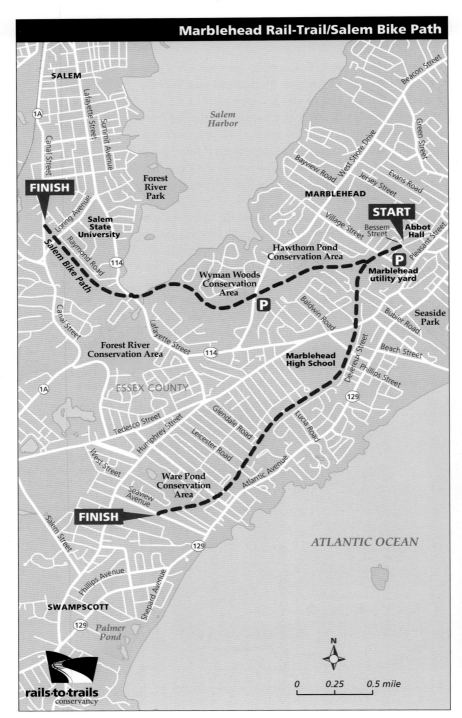

Marblehead Rail-Trail/Salem Bike Path

SALEM

1A

Lafayette Street

Summit Avenue

Canal Street

Salem Harbor

Beacon Street

Green Street

West Shore Drive

Bayview Road

Jersey Street

Evans Road

Forest River Park

MARBLEHEAD

Village Street

FINISH

Loring Avenue

Salem State University

Raymond Road

114

Salem Bike Path

START

Bessem Street

Abbot Hall

Pleasant Street

Hawthorn Pond Conservation Area

P

Marblehead utility yard

Wyman Woods Conservation Area

P

Bubier Road

Seaside Park

Canal Street

Baldwin Road

Devereux Street

Beach Street

Lafayette Street

Forest River Conservation Area

114

Marblehead High School

Phillips Street

1A

ESSEX COUNTY

129

Tedesco Street

Glendale Road

Lucia Road

Humphrey Street

Leicester Road

West Street

Ware Pond Conservation Area

Atlantic Avenue

Seaview Avenue

FINISH

ATLANTIC OCEAN

Salem Street

129

Phillips Avenue

Shepard Avenue

SWAMPSCOTT

129

Palmer Pond

N

0   0.25   0.5 mile

rails·to·trails
conservancy

The junction at the old station site in downtown Marblehead is a central starting point with plenty of parking. It's only a few blocks from the town's historical waterfront, where fishing and whaling ships docked alongside privateers during the American Revolution. Reflecting the spirit of those times, the distinctive Abbot Hall museum on Washington Street displays *The Spirit of '76*, a painting depicting a fife and drum corps marching across a battlefield.

Follow the sandy path across from Round House Road for 0.25 mile to a utility yard, and take the right fork toward Salem. The sandy trail enters the 10-acre Hawthorn Pond Conservation Area, where you'll find marshes, ponds, and nature trails. Crossing West Shore Drive, you enter the 34-acre Wyman Woods Conservation Area to find more wetlands and hardwood forests alongside Salem Harbor. Trail users can hike down a sandy footpath to the water's edge or view the scenic harbor from a bridge.

Use caution crossing busy MA 114/Lafayette Street to a smooth asphalt section of the trail labeled Salem Bike Path. This 0.6-mile segment ends at Canal Street after passing Salem State University. Another 0.6-mile section between Canal and Roslyn Streets is scheduled for construction in 2018 to connect with an existing short segment that ends at Mill Street. The MBTA Salem Station, Salem Old Town Hall, the harbor, and museums related to the witch trials are all close by.

Taking the left fork at the Marblehead utility yard, you'll head toward Swampscott, nearly 2 miles away. The sand and gravel trail crosses Pleasant Street and runs beside playing fields at Marblehead High School. Students from nearby homes use the trail as a commuter route. About 0.5 mile past the Temple Emanu-El parking lot, the trail passes a side path to the 9-acre Ware Pond Conservation Area, where you can visit the pond and wildlife refuge on nature trails.

The trail becomes a narrow path before it ends on Seaview Avenue at the Swampscott town limits. Residents voted in 2017 to design a 2-mile extension along the old railroad right-of-way to the MBTA Swampscott Station, where the 1868 Eastern Railroad station is located.

CONTACT: marblehead.org/about-marblehead/pages/hidden-town-jewels and salem.com/bicycling-advisory-committee

DIRECTIONS

To reach the Marblehead trailhead from MA 128/Yankee Division Hwy., take Exit 26 for Lowell St. Head east on Lowell St., which becomes Main St. in Peabody, then Boston St. Go 2.5 miles and turn right onto MA 107/Essex St. and then in 0.1 mile turn left onto Jackson St. Go 0.4 mile and turn right onto Jefferson Ave., and then go 1.2 miles and turn left onto MA 1A/Loring Ave. Go 0.5 mile and turn right onto MA 114/Lafayette St. Go 1.3 miles and turn left onto W. Shore Dr., and then go 0.8 mile and turn right onto Village St. Go 0.4 mile and turn left onto Highland Ter., which curves right to become Bessom St. Look for parking on either side of Round House Road.

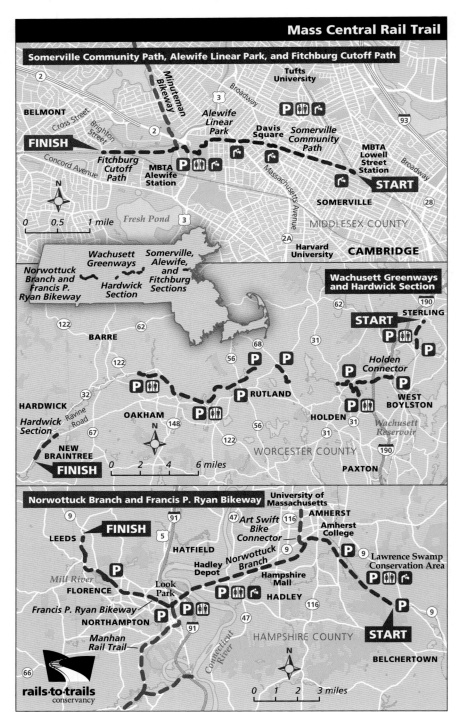

Mass Central Rail Trail

Somerville Community Path, Alewife Linear Park, and Fitchburg Cutoff Path

Wachusett Greenways and Hardwick Section

Norwottuck Branch and Francis P. Ryan Bikeway

rails·to·trails
conservancy

The Massachusetts Central Railroad was destroyed by a hurricane in 1938, but the 104-mile corridor is being reborn as a cross-state rail-trail. Currently, more than 30 miles from Boston to Northampton have been converted to trails, often by dedicated local groups that are piecing together this important part of the Bay State's history. Here, we outline the open segments of the Mass Central Rail Trail from east to west.

Somerville Community Path, Alewife Linear Park, and Fitchburg Cutoff Path

The easternmost section of the Mass Central Rail Trail offers a seamless paved route connecting the Somerville Community Path, the Alewife Linear Park, and the

The Norwottuck Branch of the trail crosses the Connecticut River on a spectacular trestle in Northampton.

Counties
Hampshire, Middlesex, Worcester

Endpoints
Lowell St. at Maxwells Green (Somerville) to Brighton St. just south of Vale Road (Belmont); Waushacum Ave. between Bird St. and School St. (Sterling) to Creamery Road, just east of MA 32/Lower Road (Hardwick); Warren Wright Road, 0.3 mile north of Wilson Road (Belchertown), to S. Main St., 0.1 mile south of Fort Hill Road (Leeds)

Mileage
38.0

Type
Rail-Trail/Rail-with-Trail

Roughness Index
1–2

Surfaces
Asphalt, Cinder, Crushed Stone, Dirt, Gravel

I-190 towers above the Wachusett Greenways Section in the Holden area.

Fitchburg Cutoff Path in Boston's northwestern suburbs. This unique rail-trail follows an old railway corridor aboveground while commuter trains run in a subway tunnel below. The Boston & Lowell Railroad built this spur in the 1870s, and it was later acquired by the Boston and Maine Railroad. The Massachusetts Bay Transportation Authority (MBTA) purchased the line in 1973 and began using it for commuter trains in the 1980s.

The route begins at MBTA's planned Green Line station on Lowell Street in Somerville. Heading northwest from there, you'll approach the hip Davis Square area after 0.8 mile. Many buildings date to the late 1800s in this district, which is a destination for shopping, dining, and nightlife. Given its proximity to Tufts and Harvard Universities, it has a strong arts and culture vibe. If you're traveling by bicycle, you'll have to dismount (or take alternative on-street routes) as you approach Seven Hills Park and Davis Square, as cycling is prohibited on the path in this congested area.

In a mile, you'll reach Alewife Station. This section gets a lot of use as it connects with the popular Minuteman Bikeway (see page 125) near the station. The trail continues as a tree-lined pathway to its end at Brighton Street on the eastern border of Belmont.

Wachusett Greenways Section (Sterling to Barre)

About 50 miles west of Boston, this section of the Mass Central Rail Trail includes a handful of completed—but disconnected—trail segments in a smattering of charming communities between Sterling and Barre. A nonprofit volunteer group called Wachusett Greenways is spearheading the effort to knit these pieces together.

Begin your journey in Sterling at the shared parking lot of the Cider Mill Shops. The scenic, crushed-stone pathway heads south through wetlands and oak-pine forest. After 1.3 miles, you'll cross a small bridge and ride along a berm between two bodies of water, West Waushacum Pond on one side and The Quag on the other. This popular fishing spot is noted for its abundance of both smallmouth and largemouth bass. In 0.3 mile, the trail ends at Gates Road; on the opposite side of the road, a parking lot is available.

A short gap of 3.5 miles lies between trail's end and the next section of trail, locally known as the Holden Connector, which begins to the southeast in West Boylston. A note of caution: This section often deviates from the original rail corridor with uphill sections and terrain that could pose a bit of challenge for those not on mountain bikes. From the parking area on Thomas Street, the route follows the wooded banks of the Quinapoxet River for 2.7 miles to River Street, opening up when the trail passes under I-190. Along the way, benches provide tranquil spots to rest.

When you reach the trailhead parking lot on River Street, the route pivots and heads northwest. The trail here is more challenging with steep turns and loose gravel and dirt, best suited for hiking or sturdy all-terrain bicycles. In 0.9 mile you'll cross Manning Street and continue uphill through the dense canopy; this portion of the trail borders private land, so please be courteous. Your adventure ends in 1.1 miles at Wachusett Street in Holden, where another trail parking lot is available. Cross Wachusett Street and you can continue riding on-road along Mill Street for 0.9 mile south to view Lovellville Falls and the remains of a mill on the Asnebumskit Brook. Though not marked as a bike route, it's a quiet, wooded street.

The trail picks up again in Rutland, about 5 miles to the west. The unpaved trail parallels East County Road for 1.2 miles with a parking lot on its northern end on Wachusett Street. An on-road route will connect you to the next section of trail. From the parking lot, ride on Wachusett southwest 1.3 miles and turn right onto Glenwood Road; in 0.6 mile, you'll be at the next trailhead. From the Glenwood Road parking lot, you'll have a pleasant journey heading southwest through forested conservation areas with wetlands and ponds, offering many opportunities for viewing local wildlife. About 2.5 miles into the trip, you'll find yourself surrounded by the spectacular rocky cliffs that the railway cut through, offering a nice bit of natural air-conditioning on a hot summer day. Nearing the end of this section of trail, you'll cross busy MA 122/Worcester Road; traffic moves at high speeds here, so use caution and listen for the rumble strips as a warning for oncoming vehicles. The trail soon parallels the Ware River before coming to an end at a spacious parking area next to MA 122 near Barre.

Hardwick Section

This 3-mile section of trail runs through open fields and deep woods in the heart of Massachusetts. The trail crosses the Ware River on two bridges restored by local trail managers and volunteers, including a lattice-truss trestle, similar in design but smaller in scale to the Norwottuck Branch's span over the Connecticut River.

The pathway surface is largely packed dirt, suitable for people on foot, mountain bike, or horseback. In the winter, cross-country skiers and snowmobilers can be seen enjoying the trail. It runs between Maple Street in Wheelwright to Creamery Road in Hardwick. The best parking location for this section of trail is near the eastern endpoint at the site of a former train station in New Braintree, between Hardwick Road and West Road.

Norwottuck Branch (Belchertown to Northampton)

The Norwottuck Branch of the Mass Central Rail Trail (formerly known as the Norwottuck Rail Trail) stretches 10 miles from Belchertown to Northampton, connecting Hadley and Amherst in between. Trees border most of the pathway, providing a shaded journey through the summer heat and beautiful foliage in the fall. The trail has secluded spots to enjoy wildlife, as well as more well-used areas near Amherst College and the University of Massachusetts and into the city of Northampton, where the trail crosses the Connecticut River on a spectacular trestle.

Beginning your journey at the easternmost endpoint at the Warren Wright Road trailhead, you'll travel through wetlands bordering the Lawrence Swamp Conservation Area. Views of streams and water lily–laden waterways can be seen through the forested corridor along the trail. Several hiking paths through this protected area, including the famed Robert Frost Trail, branch from the rail-trail and allow a closer look at the wildlife and wetlands. Before leaving the Lawrence Swamp area, you'll pass through Lawrence Station, with several picnic benches, a portable restroom, parking, and an information kiosk.

The paved pathway continues under a leafy canopy. You'll come upon the Fort River access point, which leads to the Emily Dickinson Trail (hiking only).

Parking is available here just to the south of the trail at Mill Lane. About 4 miles in, the pathway arches into Amherst, rolling by the sports fields of Amherst College. As you head south, the trail intersects with the Art Swift Bike Connector, which leads northward to the University of Massachusetts campus.

The route continues west to Hadley through a mixture of farmlands and busier spots, like the commercial areas around Hampshire Mall and Mountain Farms Mall. Just off the trail around the Hadley Depot trailhead is an art gallery and an eclectic bar/restaurant with vintage arcade games, complete with a trailside Pac-Man–themed bike rack.

As you head into Northampton, you'll cross over a lattice-truss bridge, an impressive steel structure with beautiful views of the Connecticut River. A park with docks and river access lies at the western end of the bridge.

At Woodmont Road, this section of the Mass Central Rail Trail connects to its Francis P. Ryan Bikeway section by way of a tunnel under an active rail line; the underpass opened in November 2017. At this intersection, the trail also connects with the Manhan Rail Trail (see page 112), which heads south through downtown Northampton.

Francis P. Ryan Bikeway

The paved pathway continues northwest toward Look Park, running through residential and commercial areas in Northampton and the village of Florence. Along the way, tree canopy shades much of the trail, making for a pleasant walk or ride even in hot weather. A trailside bike repair station, just after crossing Straw Avenue, provides free air and basic tools for bicyclists. Upon arriving at Look Park, a 150-acre privately operated, nonprofit park, consider taking a break to ride the miniature train around a 1-mile track, visit the zoo, or rent a paddleboat at the lake. The trail skirts the perimeter of the park to the east.

Heading past Look Park, the trail enters the woods, continuing through heavy forest alongside the rushing water of Mill River. After a while, the path changes from an asphalt surface to packed cinder—and back to asphalt and then again to cinder farther along; both surfaces are suitable for all types of bikes. Along the trail, the river is not always within view, but the sound of laughter can be heard on hot days, where numerous unofficial swimming holes attract those wanting to splash in the cool water. The trail ends at South Main Street, a rural road not recommended for bicycling, adjacent to a bridge over Mill River in the village of Leeds.

CONTACT: masscentralrailtrail.org, wachusettgreenways.org, and fntg.net

DIRECTIONS

As the Mass Central Rail Trail spans much of Massachusetts, there are numerous parking options. Below are a few key parking waypoints; please visit the trail websites listed here or **TrailLink.com** for more options.

Cambridge: By MBTA subway, take the Red Line to the Alewife Station. Bicycles are permitted on subways on weekends and during off-peak hours on weekdays (visit **mbta.com/bikes /bike-rules**). A Hubway bike-share station is located at the Alewife Station (**thehubway.com**).

To reach parking (fee charged) at the Alewife Station from I-95, take Exit 29A to MA 2 toward Boston. Go 5.9 miles and take the Alewife Station exit. The Alewife Station Access Road becomes Steel Place. Go 0.4 mile and turn left into the parking garage. For more information, visit **mbta.com.**

Sterling: To reach the northern endpoint from I-90, take Exit 6 for MA 12 toward Sterling/ Clinton. Head south on MA 12/Leominster Road (signs for Sterling/Clinton), and go 1.7 miles. Continue straight onto MA 12 S/MA 62 W for 0.2 mile. Turn left onto Waushacum Ave. The entrance to trail parking will be on the right in 0.2 mile; look for an old red shed just off the road.

Holden: To reach the parking area at the Wachusett Reservoir on Thomas St. from I-190, take Exit 5 for MA 140 toward West Boylston. Head south on MA 140. In 0.9 mile, keep right to stay on Thomas St. The parking lot will be on your right.

Rutland: To reach the Wachusett St. trailhead from I-190, take Exit 5 to MA 140 toward West Boylston. Head south on MA 140 about 1 mile, and turn right onto Laurel St. Continue 3.3 miles (Laurel St. becomes Manning St.). Turn left onto MA 31. In 0.25 mile, turn right onto Quinapoxet St. In 2 miles turn right onto Main St./MA 122A. In 3 miles, turn right onto Glenwood Road. In 1.2 miles, the parking area will be on your right.

Hardwick: To reach the parking area at the eastern end of the trail from I-90, take Exit 8 for MA 32, then turn left onto MA 32/Thorndike St. In 8.4 miles, turn right at Main St./MA 9 in Ware to continue on MA 32. In 1.7 miles, turn left onto Gilbertville Road to continue on MA 32 (just past a recycling facility on your left). In 3.4 miles, you'll turn right in Gilbertville to stay on MA 32. In another 3.7 miles, turn right onto Hardwick Road. Just past West Road, in 0.3 mile, turn right. The parking area will be a mowed grassy area on your right.

Norwottuck Branch: To reach the Warren Wright Road trailhead in Belchertown from I-91 N, take Exit 19 and turn right onto MA 9/Bridge St., eastbound over the Connecticut River. After crossing the river, turn right onto Bay Road. Continue 1.8 miles and turn left to stay on Bay Road. After 3 miles, take the second exit on the traffic circle just past Atkins Farms Country Market onto MA 116, then almost immediately take the first exit at the next traffic circle to continue on Bay Road. In 2.5 miles, veer left onto Hulst Road. In just under a mile, turn left onto Warren Wright Road. In 0.8 mile, the trailhead parking area will be on your left, just before the train tracks.

Many commuters choose the Minuteman Bikeway for freedom from congested traffic in the northwest Boston suburbs. For others, the 10.1-mile paved trail between Cambridge and Bedford serves as a historical route through the opening salvos of the American Revolution. The rail-trail roughly traces Paul Revere's midnight ride in April 1775 to warn local militias about advancing British troops. Today, it connects a rapid transit station in Cambridge with Arlington, Lexington, and Bedford.

The rail-trail uses a corridor first laid out in the 1840s for the Lexington & West Cambridge Railroad, which later became the Boston & Lowell Railroad in 1870 and the Boston and Maine Railroad in 1887. The Massachusetts Bay Transportation Authority (MBTA) bought the line in 1976, shutting down passenger service in 1977 and freight service in 1981. The rail-trail opened in 1993 and joined Rails-to-Trails Conservancy's Rail-Trail Hall of Fame in 2008.

Starting at the MBTA Alewife Station in Cambridge (bikes are allowed on Red Line trains in off-peak hours), you'll immediately pass the Alewife Linear Park trail that heads east toward Somerville and the Fitchburg Cutoff

Bedford Depot Park commemorates railroad history with a vintage depot freight house and a restored passenger rail car.

County
Middlesex

Endpoints
MBTA Alewife Station at Alewife Station Access Road at Concord Turnpike/MA 2 (Cambridge) to Bedford Depot Park at South Road and Loomis St. (Bedford)

Mileage
10.1

Type
Rail-Trail

Roughness Index
1

Surface
Asphalt

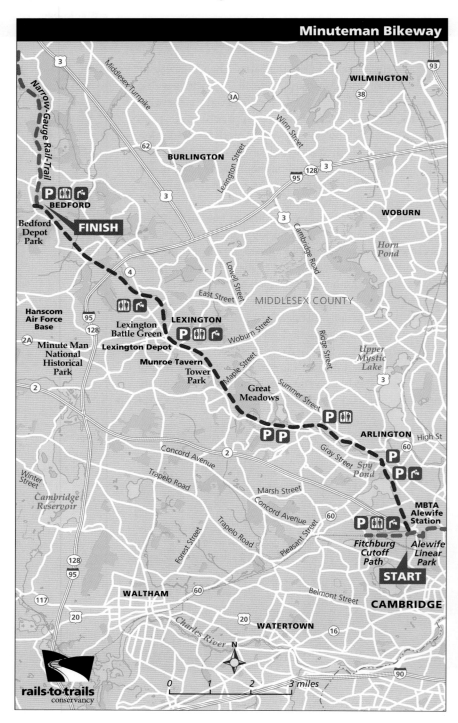

Path heading west (both part of the Mass Central Rail Trail; see page 118). The trail passes the 100-acre Spy Pond in Arlington before arriving at a short, on-road section in historic Arlington Center at mile 1.5. Here, follow the signs, bike lanes, and pedestrian signals to cross Swan Place, Massachusetts Avenue/US 3, and Mystic Street/MA 60 to regain the bikeway on the north side of the intersection.

Trailside displays tell the history of these first battles of the Revolutionary War. One of the first is in Arlington (named Menotomy in Colonial times), where you'll learn about the Battle at the Foot of the Rocks located just a couple of blocks off the trail. About 3 miles later in Arlington, you'll pass the 183-acre Great Meadows, followed by the Tower Park picnic grounds—both sites of Revolutionary battles—and the Munroe Tavern, used as a headquarters during the conflict.

The Lexington Visitor Center sits next to the trail, which is a block away from Lexington Battle Green, where minutemen resisted British soldiers. The trail veers away from Massachusetts Avenue as it leaves Lexington and becomes a wooded corridor through quiet neighborhoods for its last 3.7 miles to Bedford Depot Park. Railroad history is celebrated here at a vintage depot freight house and a restored passenger rail car. The trail meets the northbound Narrow-Gauge Rail-Trail (see page 128) across Loomis Street. In the planning stages, an extension of the Minuteman Bikeway will continue west along Railroad Avenue for 0.3 mile to meet the Reformatory Branch Trail (see page 157) toward Concord.

The trail can be congested with bicyclists during morning and evening commutes and with pedestrians on weekends and lunch hours. Local laws require that bicyclists dismount when using sidewalks in city centers. Restaurants, pubs, markets, and bike shops are located close to the path.

CONTACT: minutemanbikeway.org

DIRECTIONS

To reach the Cambridge trailhead by subway, take the MBTA Red Line to the Alewife Station. Bicycles are allowed on weekends and during off-peak hours on weekdays; see **mbta.com** for details. A Hubway bike-share station is located at the Alewife Station (**thehubway.com**). Pick up the trail on the north side of the terminal.

To reach the Cambridge trailhead by car from I-95, take Exit 29A to MA 2 toward Boston. Go 5.9 miles and take the Alewife Station exit. The Alewife Station Access Road becomes Steel Place. Go 0.4 mile and turn left into the parking garage (fee charged). The trail starts on the north side of the building.

To reach Bedford Depot Park from I-95, take Exit 31B onto MA 4 N/MA 225 W toward Bedford. Turn right, and go 1.8 miles. Turn left onto Loomis St. In 0.3 mile look for Bedford Depot Park on the left and turn into the parking lot. The trail starts at the locomotive display at the west end of the park.

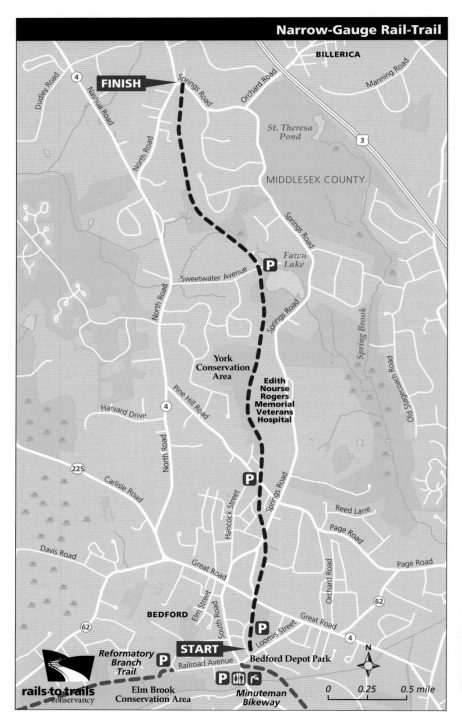

Narrow-Gauge Rail-Trail

BILLERICA

Dudley Road

Nashua Road

4

FINISH

Springs Road

Orchard Road

Manning Road

North Road

St. Theresa
Pond

3

MIDDLESEX COUNTY

Springs Road

P

Fawn
Lake

Sweetwater Avenue

North Road

Springs Road

Spring Brook

Old Stagecoach Road

York
Conservation
Area

Pine Hill Road

Edith
Nourse
Rogers
Memorial
Veterans
Hospital

Harvard Drive

4

North Road

225

Carlisle Road

P

Springs Road

Reed Lane

Page Road

Davis Road

Hancock Street

Great Road

Orchard Road

Page Road

62

BEDFORD

Elm Street

South Road

P

Loomis Street

Great Road

4

62

Reformatory
Branch
Trail

P

START

Bedford Depot Park

N

Railroad Avenue

P

Elm Brook
Conservation Area

Minuteman
Bikeway

0   0.25   0.5 mile

rails·to·trails
conservancy

Even though the Narrow-Gauge Rail-Trail traces the nation's first narrow-gauge railroad for 3 miles from Bedford toward Billerica, the mostly crushed-stone path is plenty wide enough now to accommodate people passing on foot or bicycle.

The trail follows the route of the Billerica & Bedford Railroad, built in 1877 with a narrow 2-foot-wide track to save money on construction costs. The company soon went bankrupt anyway, and in 1885 the Boston & Lowell Railroad used the corridor to build a standard-gauge railroad. The tracks went out of use in 1962, and the town of Bedford purchased its share of the right-of-way to build a 10-foot-wide trail. The town of Billerica is seeking funds to do the same for a future trail tentatively named Yankee Doodle Bike Path.

The route starts across Loomis Street from Bedford Depot Park, where it meets the Minuteman Bikeway (see

Fawn Lake highlights the north end of the route.

County
Middlesex

Endpoints
Loomis St. between Hartford St. and DeAngelo Dr. (Bedford) to Springs Road at Astrig Way (Billerica)

Mileage
3.0

Type
Rail-Trail

Roughness Index
2

Surfaces
Asphalt, Crushed Stone, Dirt

page 125). An old railroad building that served as an engine house for the Billerica & Bedford Railroad and later as a freight house for the Boston and Maine Railroad has been restored there and is open on weekends April–October with displays of railroad memorabilia. Park visitors also can see a restored diesel passenger car that ran on the line.

The first 0.3 mile of the trail to MA 4/Great Road is paved, but the rest is stone dust. Mountain or hybrid bikes are recommended for this surface. Use caution at this road crossing as a commercial district is located nearby.

Entering a wooded residential area, you'll pass the former site of a passenger station on Springs Road. The trail passes the sprawling Edith Nourse Rogers Memorial Veterans Hospital (built in 1928) on the right about a mile past MA 4/Great Road. The York Conservation Area on the left offers a welcome stop for a picnic on the green or a stroll around the pond. Bikes are not permitted on paths in the conservation area, but you can explore on foot.

Sweetwater Avenue crosses the trail about 0.8 mile past the hospital. The former site of the Bedford Springs Station, nearby Fawn Lake served as a health resort for well-to-do visitors from Boston and New York in the late 19th century. A self-guided path encircles the pond. The trail ends at Springs Road, just across the Billerica town line.

CONTACT: bedforddepot.org

DIRECTIONS

To reach the trailhead at Bedford Depot Park from I-95, take Exit 31B onto MA 4 N/MA 225 W toward Bedford. Turn right, and go 1.8 miles. Turn left onto Loomis St. Go 0.4 mile and turn left into the park just past Hartford St. on the right. The trail starts at the northeast end of the park at a crosswalk across Loomis St.

To reach parking near the north end of the trail from I-95, take Exit 31B onto MA 4 N/MA 225 W toward Bedford. Turn right, and go 2.6 miles. Bear right onto MA 4/North Road, and then go 1.3 miles and turn right onto Sweetwater Ave. Go 0.4 mile and look for parking on the right, just past the trail crossing. The trail ends 1.1 miles north on Springs Road.

The Nashua River Rail Trail stretches from southern Nashua, New Hampshire, to downtown Ayer, Massachusetts, connecting to the towns of Pepperell and Groton. The trail is built on the former rail corridor of the Hollis Branch of the Boston and Maine Railroad. The last freight line to run on the rails was in 1982. Now, trail users of all ages and abilities can be seen along the rail-trail. Deciduous forests border most of the path, offering spectacular views of fall foliage and providing shaded travels in the spring and summer. The pathway winds through several wetlands and

The pathway winds through several wetlands and waterways, including passage over Groton School Pond.

Counties
Hillsborough (NH),
Middlesex (MA)

Endpoints
Gilson Road at Country
Side Dr. (Nashua, NH) to
Main St. between Park St.
and West St. (Ayer, MA)

Mileage
12.4

Type
Rail-Trail

Roughness Index
1

Surface
Asphalt

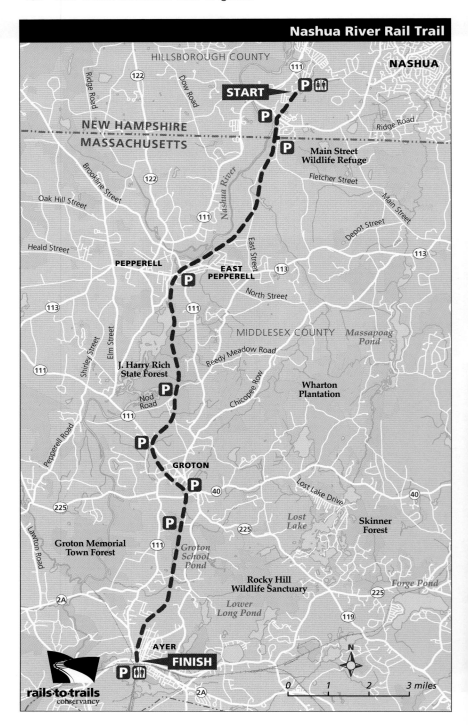

Nashua River Rail Trail

waterways, with ample opportunities to take in the view and see turtles, birds, and other wildlife along the way.

From the northern endpoint in Nashua, New Hampshire, the trail begins next to a small pond in a residential area and heads south into a forested area. In about a mile, you'll reach the Massachusetts state line, followed by the town of Pepperell, Massachusetts, in another 3.2 miles. The trail opens up into a small trailside plaza in East Pepperell with a town clock, bike maintenance station, and signage celebrating town hero Colonel William Prescott, who is attributed with saying, "Do not fire until you see the whites of their eyes!" at the Battle of Bunker Hill.

Several shops line Main Street across from the plaza. If you have time, head north on Groton Street to see the historical covered bridge that crosses the Nashua River. At a small park on the east bank of the river, you can learn about the exploits of Prudence Wright, considered to be the first American woman to hold—and receive pay for—a military title.

The route continues past Pepperell Dam on the Nashua River. Pepperell Pond, behind the dam, is a well-known fishing spot for largemouth and smallmouth bass and often hosts fishing tournaments. This portion of the trail borders the J. Harry Rich State Forest—a great place to explore on foot with several hiking and horseback riding trails and excellent river views. The forest can be accessed off Sand Hill/Nod Road near the trail parking area.

The scenic path is truly multiuse, enjoyed by walkers, bicyclists, in-line skaters, equestrians, and others.

Just over a mile later, a small railway bridge over Main Street brings you into Groton, Massachusetts. The landscape soon changes from forest to vast meadows. A mile farther, you'll come upon Groton School Pond. This is a great resting spot, with rough-hewn granite benches and views of both forest and farmland. The pond is rich with fish, turtles, birds, and other wildlife.

The mix of forest and meadow views continues into the town of Ayer, where the trail ends at Main Street. Visit the downtown area for a taste of its past as a major railway hub and Civil War army training camp.

Other nearby trails surround the Nashua River Rail Trail, especially at the northern endpoint in Nashua, New Hampshire. This endpoint is less than 5 miles south from the southern tip of the 6-mile Nashua Canal Trail (Mine Falls Park), as well as the southern endpoint of the 1.3-mile Nashua Heritage Rail-Trail.

CONTACT: mass.gov/eea/agencies/dcr/massparks/region-central/nashua-river -rail-trail.html

DIRECTIONS

To reach the northern trailhead in Nashua, New Hampshire, from US 3, take Exit 5 for NH 111 W toward Pepperell, Massachusetts (about 14 miles north of Lowell, Massachusetts, and 15 miles south of Manchester, New Hampshire). Use the right two lanes to take Exit 5, merging onto NH 111 W/W. Hollis St. toward Pepperell, Massachusetts. Continue on W. Hollis St. 3.3 miles, then turn left onto Country Side Dr. The trail parking lot will be at the end of Country Side Dr.

To reach the trail access and parking area in East Pepperell, Massachusetts, from US 3, take Exit 35 to head west on MA 113 toward Dunstable, Massachusetts (about 21.5 miles south of Manchester, New Hampshire, and 7.5 miles north of Lowell, Massachusetts). Head west on Kendall Road/MA 113 W. Continue on MA 113 W 2.4 miles, then turn left to stay on MA 113 W. Stay on MA 113 W another 5 miles, then turn right onto Groton St. In a few hundred feet, make a left onto Main St. Parking is immediately to the left.

To reach the trail access and parking area at Sand Hill Road in Groton, Massachusetts (near the J. Harry Rich State Forest), from I-495, take Exit 31 for MA 119 toward Groton/Acton. Merge onto MA 119 W/Great Road toward Groton (right from I-495 N, left from I-495 S). Continue 7 miles, then turn right onto Hollis St. In 0.5 mile, turn left onto Common St. In 1 mile, turn right onto Sand Hill Road. In 0.25 mile, the parking lot will be on your right.

To reach the southern trailhead in Ayer, Massachusetts, from I-495, take Exit 29B for MA 2/George W. Stanton Hwy. toward Leominster. Head west on MA 2, and in 4.1 miles, take Exit 38B and merge right onto MA 110/MA 111 toward Ayer/Groton. After about 2 miles, you'll come to a traffic circle. Take the third exit onto Harvard Road. Keep right to merge onto Main St. In just over 1 mile, turn right onto Park St. In 0.15 mile turn right onto Groton St., where the parking area will be immediately on your right.

The Neponset River Greenway is a south Boston jewel, utilizing the best in design and construction standards as it winds through the Neponset River valley, offering a low-stress, high-quality experience.

American Indians used the Neponset (meaning "harvest river") for fishing and as a fur trading route with settlers arriving in the 1600s. The river played an important role in the development of Milton and Boston, though it was an early obstacle to settlers. There are several well-designed access points to the river if you decide to explore

From the north end of the trail, you can look across the Neponset River for views of downtown Boston.

County
Suffolk

Endpoints
Brush Hill Road and Neponset Valley Pkwy. (Readville) to Tenean Beach at Conley St. and I-93/MA 3/US 1 (Dorchester)

Mileage
8.2

Type
Rail-Trail/Rail-with-Trail

Roughness Index
1

Surfaces
Asphalt, Concrete

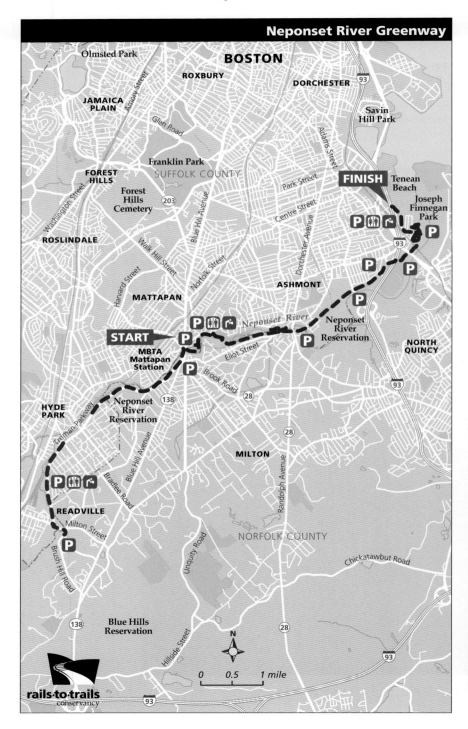

Neponset River Greenway

Olmsted Park

BOSTON

ROXBURY

DORCHESTER 93

JAMAICA
PLAIN

Amory Street

Glen Road

Savin
Hill Park

Adams Street

Franklin Park

FOREST
HILLS
SUFFOLK COUNTY

Forest
Hills
Cemetery 203

Washington Street

Blue Hill Avenue

Walk Hill Street

Park Street

Centre Street

FINISH Tenean
Beach

Joseph
Finnegan
Park

P 🏢 🚻 ⛵ P

93

ROSLINDALE

Harvard Street

Norfolk Street

MATTAPAN

ASHMONT

Dorchester Avenue

P 🏢 🚻 ⛵ *Neponset River*

P

P

P

P

Neponset
River
Reservation

START P

MBTA
Mattapan
Station

Eliot Street

P

**NORTH
QUINCY**

93

P

Brook Road

**HYDE
PARK**

Neponset
River
Reservation

Truman Parkway

138

28

28

MILTON

Randolph Avenue

P 🏢 🚻 ⛵

Blue Hill Avenue

Bradlee Road

READVILLE

Milton Street

NORFOLK COUNTY

Brush Hill Road

P

Unquity Road

Chickatawbut Road

138

**Blue Hills
Reservation**

Hillside Street

N

28

93

0   0.5   1 mile

rails·to·trails
conservancy

93

this riparian corridor by kayak or canoe, both excellent choices. If you prefer to run, walk, or skate—or if you have a foldable bike—you can take one of the Massachusetts Bay Transportation Authority (MBTA) trolleys that run along the trail's southern stretch every few minutes.

Unless you are a very experienced rider who doesn't mind riding in occasional traffic along the Truman Parkway and sharing rough and narrow sidewalks with pedestrians, we suggest you start your adventure at either the northern trailhead at Tenean Beach or the MBTA Mattapan Station to the south. You can park your car for a small fee at the station. From the station, the northern endpoint of the 2-mile Pine Tree Brook/Popes Pond Path is just 1 mile away.

From the front of Mattapan Station, go to the corner of River Street and MA 28 and look for a restored old transportation building decorated with several murals located next to MA 28. The trailhead is behind this building on a boardwalk suspended along the Neponset River, with the river on your right.

Immediately you will feel the difference from the busy streets adjacent to this tree-lined river valley. In 0.3 mile, you'll cross a new bridge that takes you over the MBTA tracks. On a sunny day, the reflective colored discs and tree imagery of the fence will reflect onto the bridge's concrete deck. It's worth stopping for a bit to take in this creative art, as well as the orange and yellow trolleys zooming underneath as they approach the station's turnaround point. The bridge has a ramp connecting to another parking lot to the right of the bridge, which makes for an alternate starting point.

The trail's canopy is very dense in this southern section. The asphalt path connects to adjacent recreation fields and businesses now located in repurposed brick manufacturing buildings along this once busy industrial corridor. The building that housed the first chocolate factory in America—Baker's Chocolate— opened in 1765 on what is now the trail corridor (it eventually became General Foods Corporation and later Kraft and is now based out of another location). The trail corridor was also home to America's first commercial railway, the Granite Railway Company, which supplied granite to the Bunker Hill Monument in Boston. Many of the retaining walls and underpasses along the corridor feature walls that have been beautifully painted by the Boston Natural Areas Network.

At the halfway point, the trail goes under the MBTA tracks and spills out to the river's marshes, providing a wonderfully dramatic experience. At this point, it is now considered a rail-with-trail. From here to the end of the route, you might share the trail with some fishermen as you pass through the Neponset River Reservation, which extends from Milton to the Boston Harbor.

The path hugs the Neponset River before passing Joseph Finnegan Park on the right. The city is creating several other adjacent parks like this one, with short trail loops of their own. As Taylor Street comes to an end, turn left onto Water Street for three short blocks on residential streets to the endpoint at Tenean Beach, where you can enjoy views of downtown Boston.

CONTACT: **mass.gov/locations/lower-neponset-river-trail**

DIRECTIONS

To reach the northern trailhead at Tenean Beach from I-93/MA 3/US 1 S, take Exit 12 for MA 3A S toward Neponset/Quincy. Continue onto MA 3A S/Gallivan Blvd. 0.2 mile. Turn left toward William T. Morrissey Blvd. Continue on William T. Morrissey Blvd. just over 0.4 mile, then turn right onto Conley St., where Tenean Beach (and parking) can be found to your left.

To reach the northern trailhead at Tenean Beach from I-93/MA 3/US 1 N, take Exit 13 toward Freeport St./Dorchester. Turn left onto Victory Road. In a few hundred feet, take another left onto Freeport St., which becomes Tenean St. Go 0.4 mile, and turn left onto Conley St., where Tenean Beach (and parking) can be found to your left in 0.2 mile.

To reach parking at the MBTA Mattapan Station from I-93, take Exit 2B to head north on MA 138 for 4.5 miles toward Milton. Turn slightly left onto Blue Hills Pkwy. Go 0.1 mile. In Mattapan, turn right at the five-way intersection onto River St. at the Mattapan Station, where a parking lot is immediately to the right.

The North Central Pathway is envisioned as a trail network connecting points of interest through and between Winchendon and Gardner. Several completed sections of trail make for a lovely ride or walk between these two towns, punctuated by a stretch of less than a mile requiring travel on public roads.

Beginning at the northern endpoint in Winchendon at Clark Memorial YMCA on Summer Drive, this well-maintained asphalt trail parallels Whitney Pond before arriving at another parking lot for trail users in 0.9 mile at Glenallen Street and MA 12. Continuing east from here, the path soon enters beautiful bogs where one can easily imagine moose inhabiting—and a close eye may just see one. This stretch of trail is railroad-straight as it sits just above the shallow waters, with light tree canopy allowing the sun's rays to reach the ground.

Traveling 2 miles past Whitney Pond brings trail users to the terminus of this segment at North Ashburnham Road, where a short gap exists before the next section of designated trail. To access the next section, turn right onto North Ashburnham Road and follow it to make another right onto MA 12/Spring Street. Continue west on MA 12 approximately 800 feet and make a left onto Old Gardner Road. Continuing down Old Gardner Road about 0.5 mile leads to the trail once again.

County
Worcester

Endpoints
Summer Dr. behind Clark Memorial YMCA, 0.2 mile northeast of Beech St. (Winchendon), to Veterans Dr. and Park St. (Gardner)

Mileage
8.9

Type
Rail-Trail

Roughness Index
1

Surfaces
Asphalt, Dirt

Two beautiful bodies of water, Whitney Pond and Crystal Lake, bookend the pathway.

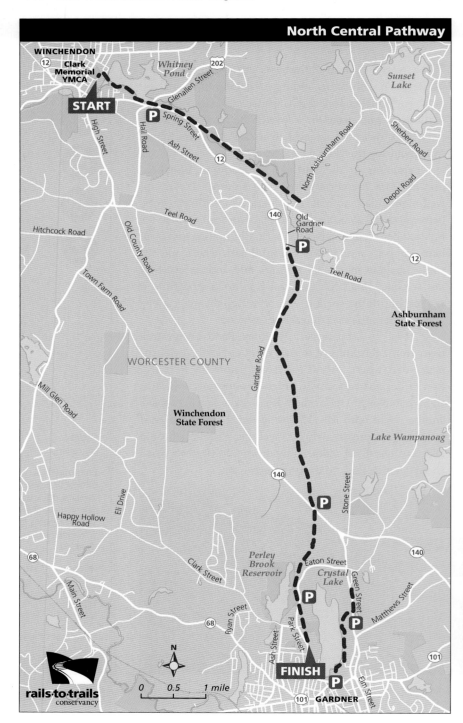

North Central Pathway

WINCHENDON
Clark Memorial YMCA
START

Whitney Pond
Sunset Lake

Glenallen Street

High Street
Hall Road
Spring Street
Ash Street

North Ashburnham Road
Sherbert Road

Teel Road
Old Gardner Road
Depot Road

Hitchcock Road
Old County Road

Town Farm Road

Ashburnham State Forest

Teel Road

WORCESTER COUNTY

Gardner Road

Winchendon State Forest

Lake Wampanoag

Mill Glen Road

Eli Drive

Happy Hollow Road

Stone Street

Perley Brook Reservoir
Eaton Street
Crystal Lake
Green Street
Matthews Street

Clark Street

Main Street

Ryan Street

Clark Street
Ash Street
Park Street

FINISH

Elm Street

GARDNER

N

0   0.5   1 mile

rails-to-trails
conservancy

Another parking lot for trail users is located at the intersection of Old Gardner Road and MA 140/Gardner Road. From this point, whether starting here or having arrived from Winchendon, the route continues as a well-maintained asphalt path through forest and bog. Approximately 2 miles from the Old Gardner Road parking lot, a trailside bike repair station with air and basic tools has been installed, along with a bench for those wishing to rest a bit. Another mile of smooth trail leads to the crossing of MA 140/Green Street, where a small parking area suitable for one or two vehicles is located.

After the MA 140 crossing, the trail turns to packed dirt suitable for many bicycles, though narrow tires may find the terrain challenging. This section of trail stretches approximately 1.5 miles, ending near Crystal Lake Cemetery in Gardner. Crystal Lake is a beautiful body of water with great views atop the cemetery. There is no parking directly at the Gardner endpoint, nor is the trail as inviting or developed as its northern endpoint in Winchendon.

Nearby trails include the 7.2-mile Monadnock Recreational Rail-Trail, just 2.2 miles north of the Winchendon endpoint; and the 1.3-mile Ashburnham Rail Trail, 5.2 miles from the small parking area at MA 140/Green Street.

CONTACT: gardner-ma.gov/facilities/facility/details/North-Central-Pathway-6

DIRECTIONS

To reach the northern endpoint behind the Clark Memorial YMCA in Winchendon from the intersection of MA 2 and US 202 in Phillipston, Massachusetts, head north on US 202 for 10 miles, and turn left onto Central St. as you approach Winchendon. Go 0.3 mile, then turn right onto Grove St. The trailhead is located behind the YMCA on Summer Dr.

To reach the northern endpoint behind the Clark Memorial YMCA in Winchendon from the intersection of NH 119 and US 202 in Rindge, New Hampshire, head south on US 202 for 5.1 miles, and turn right to remain on US 202. In another 1.7 miles, turn left onto Central St. In 0.2 mile, turn left onto Grove St. The trailhead is located behind the YMCA on Summer Dr.

To reach the parking lot at Old Gardner Road and MA 140/Gardner Road in Winchendon from the intersection of US 202 and NH 119 in Rindge, New Hampshire, head south on US 202 for 5.1 miles. Continue on Glenallen St. as you approach Winchendon. In 1.6 miles, take a sharp left onto MA 12 S/Spring St. Go 1.5 miles, then continue straight on MA 140 S for 1 mile. Turn left onto Old Gardner Road. Parking will be to your left, with the alternate trailhead across the street.

To reach the parking lot at Old Gardner Road and MA 140/Gardner Road in Winchendon from the intersection of MA 2 and US 202 in Phillipston, Massachusetts, head east on MA 2 for 10.2 miles, and take Exit 24A. Head north on W. Main St./MA 140 toward Winchendon. In 6.1 miles at Old County Road, keep right to stay on MA 140/Gardner Road. In another 2.4 miles, turn right onto Old Gardner Road. Parking will be to your left, with the alternate trailhead across the street.

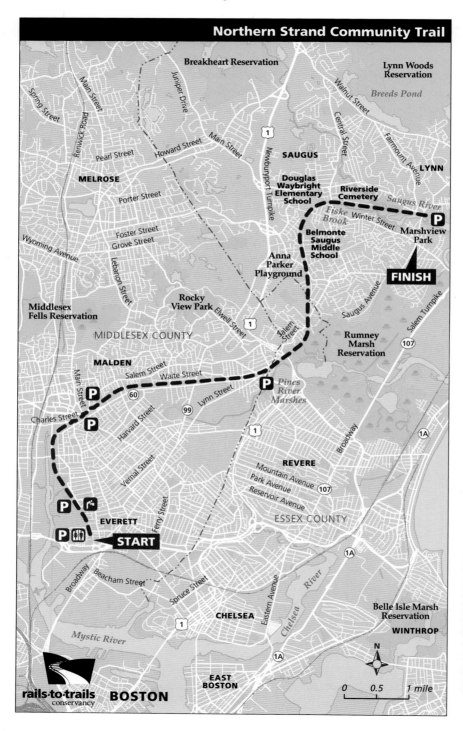

The Northern Strand Community Trail is part of the visionary and almost-complete Bike to the Sea plan to link Boston and the Mystic River to the seashore in Lynn, north of Boston. It currently runs through the cities of Everett, Malden, Revere, and the town of Saugus and provides a variety of experiences. The Saugus Branch Railroad started passenger service in 1853, and some freight moved on it until all operations stopped in 1993.

Community gardens adorn the well-loved trail.

Counties
Essex, Middlesex

Endpoints
Wellington Ave. between Cross St. and West St. (Everett) to Marshview Park at Hamilton St. and Boston St. (Lynn)

Mileage
7.6

Type
Rail-Trail

Roughness Index
1

Surfaces
Asphalt, Crushed Stone

Beginning at the southern endpoint in Everett, you'll soon see signs of the revitalization that is sweeping through both Everett and Malden. Many new high-end residential and commercial buildings, as well as adjacent parks, are under construction next to the trail. A few new brewpubs are located a few blocks off the trail in Everett, which some locals refer to as the fermentation district. Local planners and community leaders are doing an impressive job of integrating the rail-trail into this new development, providing opportunities for many lifestyles and business pursuits. Like most communities in the Boston area, drivers are courteous when approaching marked crossings, but it doesn't hurt to be cautious.

In about 1 mile, you'll reach Malden, where the smells from an adjacent bakery and coffee plant come as a wonderful surprise. Notice the well-cared-for community gardens featuring vegetables that reflect the neighborhood's diversity. Another mile farther on the left, you can visit America's largest model train store, which features an operating display on the second floor. At this point, you can see how several restaurants are reorienting themselves by constructing decks and extensions to the trail.

Also notice the gas pipeline markings on the asphalt trail. Many rail-trails do double or triple duty as they share space with utilities. At MA 60 and Beach Street—1.5 miles from the train store—you can choose from several doughnut shops. This area also has lots of free trailside parking. A few more minutes after passing US 1, the trail opens wide to the Pines River Marshes, part of the Rumney Marsh Reservation in Saugus.

A tree canopy closes in after this, and backyards are adjacent to the rail-trail. You can't miss the collection of ever-blooming plastic flowers that one neighbor on the left has planted up to the trail's edge. This part of the trail passes Anna Parker Playground on the left, where you can enjoy a treat from the farmers market on Tuesdays in the summer. The trail isn't only for summer riders, however; trail users have also been known to enjoy snowshoeing and dogsledding along the path.

With 2 miles to go until the northern endpoint, the trail crosses Essex Street at the Saugus Fire Department before taking you over Fiske Brook. In 0.3 mile from the brook, you'll pass the sports fields of Belmonte Saugus Middle School on your right and Douglas Waybright Elementary School in another 0.3 mile to your left. Once you approach Riverside Cemetery to your right, note that the last mile has occasional pea-size stone and old asphalt that should pose no problem for a hybrid bicycle. Here, you can even see and feel a bit of the railroad's history, since the old surfacing has settled a bit. White birch trees line the corridor intermittently, and an osprey nest is close by as you cross over the Saugus River.

The trip ends at the Saugus–Lynn border at Marshview Park. Note that there is limited parking at this end, with only enough room for a few cars. Looking at the marshes, trail users will see an informal footpath to the left that one day will be the completed trail to Lynn. Here, you can walk out and enjoy the marsh. Toward downtown Lynn following the Saugus River, the path is publicly owned and passable for 0.5 mile, but construction ends 0.5 mile from downtown Lynn.

CONTACT: biketothesea.com

DIRECTIONS

To reach parking near the southern trailhead in Everett from I-93 N, take Exit 29 for MA 28/MA 38, and head north on MA 28. In 1.2 miles at the traffic circle, take the fourth exit to Main St. and head northwest on Main St. toward Carter St. Go 1 mile, then turn left onto Woodville St. In 0.3 mile, parking is available at the Madeline English School, just after you pass Bell Rock St. and Woodville St. becomes Tremont St. After parking, with the school behind you, continue south on Tremont St. to Floyd St. At this point, access to the trail is on your right. Going south will take you 0.8 mile to the trailhead on Wellington Ave., whereas going north will take you to the northern endpoint in Lynn, 6.8 miles away.

To reach the northern trailhead at Marshview Park in Lynn from US 1, take the exit toward Main St./Saugus near mile 56, and follow Main St. E 0.75 mile, until it becomes Hamilton St. In another 1.2 miles, the road ends at Boston St. Marshview Park is to the right across the street.

Old Colony Rail Trail

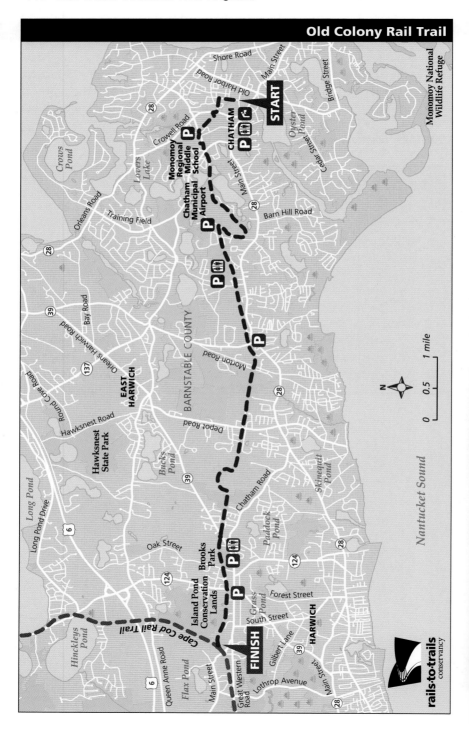

The Old Colony Rail Trail, named after the eponymous railroad line that operated in Massachusetts and Rhode Island, offers a serene journey through quiet Cape Cod beach towns. At 8 miles, the trail is suitable for a short ride out and back, or a longer journey that meets up with the Cape Cod Rail Trail (see page 88) as it extends west.

You'll want to begin your journey at the intersection of Depot Road and Hitching Post Road in Chatham, as the western endpoint in Harwich merges seamlessly with the Cape Cod Rail Trail, making it inaccessible by car. The

County
Barnstable

Endpoints
Depot Road and Hitching Post Road (Chatham) to Cape Cod Rail Trail northeast of Main St., 0.1 mile northeast of Great Western Road (Harwich)

Mileage
8.0

Type
Rail-Trail

Roughness Index
1

Surface
Asphalt

The trail makes for an easy ride with plentiful amenities nearby.

Trees buffer much of the trail, offering a serene journey through Cape Cod.

beginning of the trail features an on-road portion, but as it travels along quiet, residential streets, even inexperienced cyclists should feel safe. Follow Hitching Post Road 0.2 mile, then turn left onto Tip Cart Drive. Cross Crowell Road in another 0.2 mile and turn right to pick up the trail. Signage points the way at this junction.

You will pass through a short wooded area, emerging to cross Stepping Stones Road in 0.4 mile, where athletic facilities of Monomoy Regional Middle School are visible from the trail. In 0.3 mile, cross Old Queen Anne Road, and continue down Wilfred Road 0.6 mile via the on-street portion of the trail. Inexperienced cyclists should again face few difficulties, as this is a quiet neighborhood street with scarcely any vehicle traffic.

In 0.7 mile, the trail continues past the end of Wilfred Road, looping around Chatham Municipal Airport before pausing at George Ryder Road. Although the shoulder of this busy road functions as an on-road bicycle lane, inexperienced cyclists may wish to first dismount and then use the sidewalk as it appears. This section offers a unique view of personal, small aircraft parked at the airport, located on the right side of the sidewalk. At the next crosswalk (appearing after Northwood Road to the left), follow the signs and cross the street to pick up the trail again. Although it crosses several streets along the way, the remaining 5.4 miles of the trail remain off-road.

This section of the trail meanders through wooded backyard areas that dampen noise of the outside world. Save for the street crossings, it is easy to enjoy a quiet morning in nature, removed from the hustle and bustle of life. In 3 miles from George Ryder Road, you will pass a half-roundabout and continue along the path, passing Brooks Park and the Harwich Town Clerk on the next block, both located on the left. After crossing Pleasant Lake Avenue—1.2 miles from the half-roundabout—the trail passes Island Pond Cemetery on the right. Signage marks a cut-through to visit the Island Pond Conservation Lands, perfect for walking and hiking. The trail ends at the next roundabout and connects with the Cape Cod Rail Trail, which continues both west and north.

CONTACT: chatham-ma.gov/bikeways-committee

DIRECTIONS

To reach the Chatham endpoint from MA 28 N, head east toward Chatham until MA 28 becomes Orleans Road. About 8 miles from Orleans, turn right onto Old Harbor Road. Go 0.8 mile to the roundabout at Main St. Take the first exit onto Main St. After the gas station on the corner, take the first right possible, leading into a parking lot connected to a park complex. The trailhead is located on the other side of the park, at Depot Road toward Hitching Post Road. To reach the Chatham endpoint from MA 28 S, head east toward Chatham until MA 28 becomes Main St. About 5 miles east of Harwich port, turn left onto Depot Road. Continue 0.2 mile to Hitching Post Road. A park is located on the right and the trail is on the left.

Here, parking is available along either side of Depot Road. An additional parking lot is located on the opposite side of the park. To reach it, continue on Depot Road 0.2 mile and turn right onto Old Harbor Road. Go 0.2 mile to the roundabout at Main St. Take the first exit onto Main St. After the gas station on the corner, take the first right possible, leading into a parking lot connected to a park complex. The trailhead is located on the other side of the park, at Depot Road toward Hitching Post Road.

The terminus in Harwich is not accessible by car, as the trail joins the Cape Cod Rail Trail. The closest access point by car is a parking lot located at the intersection of Pleasant Lake Ave./MA 124 and Old Colony Road in Harwich. To reach this parking lot from US 6, take Exit 10 for MA 124 toward Harwich/Brewster. Turn right (from the east) or left (from the west) onto MA 124 S/Pleasant Lake Ave. Go about 1.5 miles to Old Colony Road. A parking lot is located across from Old Colony Road, and the trail crosses over Pleasant Lake Ave. at this point. The trail continues 0.7 mile east to the Harwich endpoint/Cape Cod Rail Trailhead and 7.2 miles west to the Chatham endpoint.

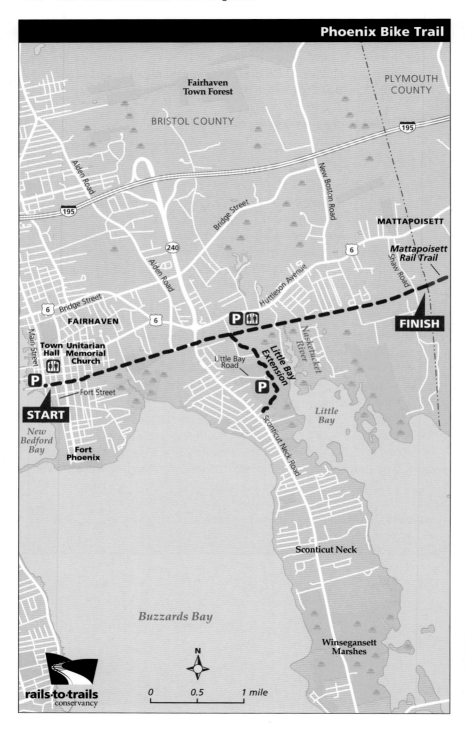

The Phoenix Bike Trail cruises through a mixture of surroundings on its relatively short 4-mile journey from the heart of the historical Fairhaven seaport to woodlands and farms on the outskirts of town. The paved rail-trail was named by schoolchildren after Fort Phoenix, less than a mile south of the downtown trailhead and within sight of the first naval battle of the American Revolution.

The trail follows the route of the Fairhaven Branch Railroad, which ran 15 miles between the ferry dock in Fairhaven through Mattapoisett to a main line connection in West Wareham. Launched in 1854, it later came under control of the New York, New Haven and Hartford Railroad from 1893 until 1953. Revived as a trail in 1999, it's the first segment of the future 50-mile South Coast Bikeway that will link Rhode Island with Cape Cod as

The trail begins in the heart of Fairhaven, which has several historical attractions near the trail.

County
Bristol

Endpoints
Main St. between Ferry St. and South St. (Fairhaven) to Mattapoisett Rail Trail between Shaw Road (Fairhaven) and Brandt Island Road (Mattapoisett)

Mileage
4.0

Type
Rail-Trail

Roughness Index
1

Surface
Asphalt

part of the East Coast Greenway, a developing trail network running from Maine to Florida.

The trail begins across Main Street from the old ferry terminal, where train passengers disembarked for the whaling and fishing center of New Bedford. The dock is used to maintain ferries serving Nantucket, Woods Hole, and Martha's Vineyard. Numerous dining establishments offer fresh seafood and ethnic fare nearby.

One block east of the trailhead, Fort Street is a good place to launch explorations of the city. If you head 1 mile south on lightly traveled Fort Street, you'll find Fort Phoenix, where reenactors fire cannons toward Buzzards Bay. From there, you can walk out on a seawall that protects New Bedford Bay from storm surges. A couple blocks north of the trail on Fort Street, you'll find a collection of ornate European-style buildings constructed by local philanthropist Henry Huttleston Rogers and donated in the late 19th century. They now serve as the Millicent Library (45 Center St.), Town Hall (40 Center St.), and the Unitarian Memorial Church (102 Green St.).

Continuing east on the trail through Fairhaven's residential area, you'll pass through the former site of the Atlas Tack factory before arriving at a modern commercial center at Sconticut Neck Road. At mile 1.6, you'll find the Little Bay Extension that forks to the right and rolls down Sconticut Neck for a mile, providing access to Little Bay along the way.

Continuing east on the Phoenix Bike Trail, you'll traverse wetlands at the head of the Nasketucket River before passing farms and pastures. Just past Shaw Road, you'll enter Plymouth County and the beginning of the Mattapoisett Rail Trail, which will one day run 4.5 miles along Buzzards Bay to the town of Mattapoisett; it's currently just over a mile in length.

CONTACT: millicentlibrary.org/phoenix-bike-trail

DIRECTIONS

To reach the Fairhaven trailhead from I-195, take Exit 18 toward MA 240 toward Fairhaven. Head south 1.1 miles and turn right onto US 6/Huttleston Ave. Go 0.3 mile and turn left onto Washington St. Go 1.0 mile and turn left onto Main St. Go 0.2 mile and turn left onto South St. for on-street parking, or right into the city parking lot at the ferry maintenance dock.

To reach the Arsene St. trailhead from I-195, take Exit 18 toward MA 240 toward Fairhaven. Head south 1.1 miles and turn left onto US 6/Huttleston Ave. Go 0.2 mile and turn right onto Arsene St. Go 0.1 mile and turn left onto an unnamed street past the Department of Public Works, which is adjacent to the trail. Take the first left into a parking lot. The eastern endpoint is 1.6 miles east, and the western endpoint is 1.9 miles west. There is no parking at the eastern endpoint.

Constructed in 1967, the Province Lands Bike Trail is the first bike trail ever built by the National Park Service. The trail features steep hills, sharp turns, and some washed-out areas, depending on the time of year. Inexperienced cyclists will want to walk their bikes in some of the steeper areas, but for those who want to enjoy nature via bike ride, the Province Lands Bike Trail is the perfect place to be. The main portion of the trail creates a loop around Beech Forest, with spurs leading to Race Point Beach, Herring Cove Beach, and a nature walking trail in Beech Forest.

Starting from the Province Lands Visitor Center, you'll want to turn left onto the trail and go almost 1 mile

Nature lovers will enjoy the Province Lands Bike Trail with its access to quiet beaches and scenic nature walks.

County
Barnstable

Endpoints
Race Point Beach at Race Point Road, 0.8 mile north of Province Lands Road, to Herring Cove Beach at Province Lands Road and MA 6A (Provincetown)

Mileage
7.7

Type
Greenway/Non-Rail-Trail

Roughness Index
1

Surface
Asphalt

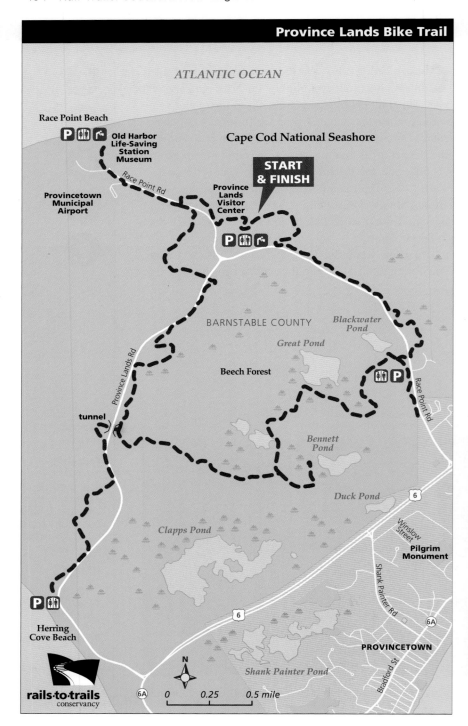

Province Lands Bike Trail

ATLANTIC OCEAN

Race Point Beach

Old Harbor Life-Saving Station Museum

Cape Cod National Seashore

START & FINISH

Province Lands Visitor Center

Provincetown Municipal Airport

Race Point Rd

BARNSTABLE COUNTY

Blackwater Pond

Great Pond

Beech Forest

Province Lands Rd

tunnel

Race Point Rd

Bennett Pond

Duck Pond

6

Clapps Pond

Winslow Street

Pilgrim Monument

Shank Painter Rd

Herring Cove Beach

6

6A

PROVINCETOWN

Bradford St

rails·to·trails
conservancy

6A   0   0.25   0.5 mile

N

Shank Painter Pond

to Race Point Beach, as perhaps one of the steepest portions of the trail is located to the right. Ups and downs are still present in this part of the trail, and scenic sand dunes point the way to Race Point Beach. The beach is worth a visit, as it also features the Old Harbor Life-Saving Station Museum, open daily 2–4 p.m. There, you may even catch a lively group of reenactors demonstrating how the U.S. Life-Saving Service carried out operations in the late 1800s.

At the Race Point Beach spur, continue onto the main loop of the trail toward Herring Cove Beach. After passing the Provincetown Municipal Airport in less than 0.25 mile to the right, the path crosses the road at a well-marked signal crossing in another 0.7 mile. The trail then continues to parallel Province Lands Road for 2.1 miles to Herring Cove Beach, crossing under the road through several low-hanging tunnels. The scenery in this section boasts sand dunes, oak trees, brush, and a wide view of the ocean on the right.

In 1 mile after crossing Province Lands Road, turn right to pass through a tunnel under the road and continue along the spur to its end at Herring Cove Beach. The route is well marked with maps and signage to help point the way. At Herring Cove Beach, you can find a seasonal concession stand, outdoor showers, and restrooms.

Continuing 1 mile from Herring Cove Beach back to the tunnel, take a right onto the main loop, heading toward Bennett Pond. Here, sandy dunes give way to pine forests in a quiet setting away from the road, with no noise from cars. In 0.8 mile from the tunnel, turn right at a short, 0.25-mile spur to reach Bennett Pond. Back on the main loop, trail users can see cranberry bogs and a lush landscape dotted with pine, birch, oak, and maple trees.

Head north on the main loop 1.2 miles to the Beech Forest parking lot and picnic area, where you'll find views of Blackwater Pond. Here, the Beech Forest Trail offers opportunities for bird-watching (note that bicycles are strictly prohibited on the soft-surface, walking-only trail).

Cross Race Point Road at another well-marked crosswalk to continue along the last 1.3-mile stretch of trail, which features a challenging up-and-down hilly section. End your journey back at the Province Lands Visitor Center, where you can read about the history and natural environment of the area—and get a glimpse of it in the observatory. History buffs might also want to explore Provincetown's Pilgrim Monument, 2 miles south of the visitor center. Its 252-foot-tall granite tower commemorates the landing of the *Mayflower* in 1620.

CONTACT: nps.gov/caco/planyourvisit/province-lands-bike-trail.htm and capecodbikeguide.com/provincelands.asp

DIRECTIONS

Four main parking areas are available within the looped Province Lands Bike Trail. To reach Herring Cove Beach from US 6, follow US 6 E to Provincetown. When US 6 ends, turn right at the fork at Herring Cove onto Province Lands Road. Go 0.1 mile. Turn left into the beach parking area, then make an immediate right. In 0.4 mile, you'll reach the end of the parking lot by the start of the trail. Note that seasonal parking fees apply.

To reach the Beech Forest Trail parking lot from US 6, follow US 6 E to Provincetown. About 0.2 mile after passing Dunes' Edge Campground on your right, turn right onto Race Point Road. In 0.5 mile, turn left into the Beech Forest Trail parking lot.

To reach the Province Lands Visitor Center from US 6, follow US 6 E to Provincetown. In about 0.2 mile after passing Dunes' Edge Campground on your right, turn right onto Race Point Road. Continue down Race Point Road 1.4 miles. At the Province Lands Visitor Center, turn right into the parking lot.

To reach Race Point Beach from US 6, follow US 6 E to Provincetown. In about 0.2 mile after passing Dunes' Edge Campground on your right, turn right onto Race Point Road. Continue down Race Point Road 1.5 miles. At Province Lands Road, bear right to continue on Race Point Road another 0.8 mile. The Race Point Beach parking lot is located at the end of the road on the right. Note that seasonal parking fees apply.

The Reformatory Branch Trail connects the historical towns of Bedford and Concord along a nearly 4-mile dirt path through wildlife refuges that ends where soldiers witnessed "the shot heard round the world" in 1775.

The trail follows a rail line built between Bedford and Concord in 1873 by the Boston & Lowell Railroad, later acquired by the Boston and Maine Railroad. Locals dubbed it the Reformatory Branch after it extended to Reformatory Station, next to a state prison, in 1879. Bedford and Concord bought the line in 1962.

Bedford Depot Park is a good place for services and connections to the Minuteman Bikeway (see page 125)

Near the west end of the trail in Concord, a side trip down Monument Street leads to the North Bridge, site of the "shot heard round the world."

County
Middlesex

Endpoints
Railroad Ave. between McMahon Road near John Glenn Middle School and Highland Ave. (Bedford) to Lowell Road at Keyes Road (Concord)

Mileage
3.9

Type
Rail-Trail

Roughness Index
2

Surface
Dirt

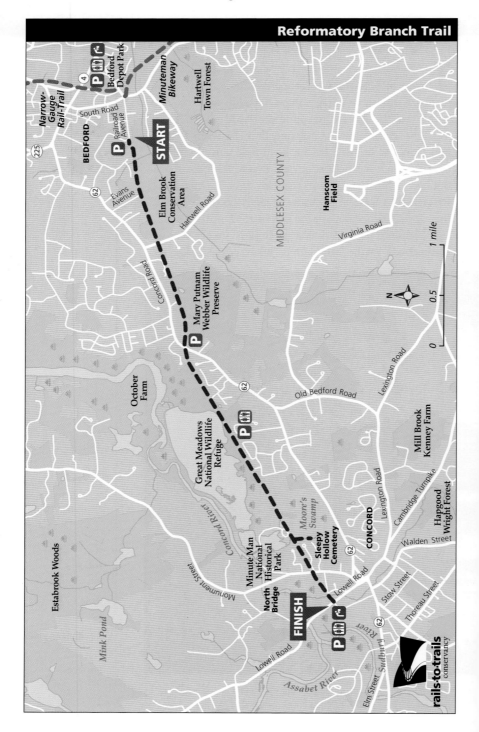

Reformatory Branch Trail

rails-to-trails
conservancy

and the Narrow-Gauge Rail-Trail (see page 128). The Bedford Freight House features railroad exhibits and photos and tours of a vintage railcar. The Reformatory Branch Trail starts at a gravel parking lot and a trailhead 0.3 mile west from the park on Railroad Avenue.

Traversing the trail by foot or mountain bike is recommended because of rough conditions. Soon after getting under way you'll reach the 19-acre Elm Brook Conservation Area and then the 20-acre Mary Putnam Webber Wildlife Preserve. Both wetlands serve as wildlife corridors for animals in the area. The trail emerges into a small gravel parking lot about 1.7 miles from the trailhead. Use caution crossing busy Concord Road/MA 62 here.

You'll enter the 3,850-acre Great Meadows National Wildlife Refuge after crossing the road. Birders flock to this freshwater wetland along the Concord and Sudbury Rivers as it's visited by 220 species of birds annually. It also shelters white-tailed deer, muskrats, red fox, raccoons, cottontail rabbits, weasels, amphibians, and several nonpoisonous snake species. Bicycles are not permitted on trails within the refuge, but you can lock your bike to one of several trailside benches and explore by foot.

Look for a Trail of the Colonial Militia stone marker about 0.9 mile past the refuge. A side path leads to Author's Ridge at Sleepy Hollow Cemetery, where you'll find the burial sites of Ralph Waldo Emerson, Henry David Thoreau, Nathaniel Hawthorne, and Louisa May Alcott, among others.

Another 0.1 mile down the path you'll cross Monument Street in Concord. A side trip to the right leads 0.2 mile to the North Bridge, site of the "shot heard round the world," the Minute Man Statue, and a visitor center. Bicycles are allowed throughout the Minute Man National Historical Park, although cyclists must dismount on the North Bridge and in many crowded locations.

The trail ends on Lowell Road. Take the crosswalk to Keyes Road, where parking and restrooms are provided at city offices during normal business hours. A trail west of these offices leads to the old trestle site across the Sudbury River and a boat launch.

Bedford is planning a future makeover for the eastern half of the former railroad corridor. The Minuteman Bikeway will be extended about 0.3 mile from Bedford Depot Park along Railroad Avenue to the Reformatory Branch Trailhead. From there, the existing dirt trail will be paved to a 12-foot-wide bikeway for 1.9 miles to the Concord city limits. The new and improved trail will be called Minuteman Bikeway Extension, but the segment in Concord will remain as it is today.

CONTACT: **bedforddepot.org** and **concordnet.org/749/Trails-Committee**

DIRECTIONS

To reach the trailhead on Railroad Ave. in Bedford from I-95, take Exit 31B onto MA 4 N/MA 225 W toward Bedford. Go 1.8 miles and turn left onto Loomis St. Go 0.4 mile and cross South Road (parking is also available at Bedford Depot Park on the left at this intersection) onto Railroad Ave. Go another 0.3 mile and look for a gravel parking lot on the left.

To reach parking for the western trailhead in Concord from I-95, take Exit 29B onto MA 2 W toward Fitchburg. The exit ramp merges onto MA 2W /Cambridge Turnpike. Go 3.1 miles and take Exit 50 to remain on Cambridge Turnpike/MA 2A E toward Lexington and Concord. Go 1.5 miles and merge onto Lexington Road. In 0.3 mile, bear right to go around Monument Square, then turn left onto Monument St. Take the immediate right turn onto Lowell Road, go 0.2 mile, and turn left onto Keyes Road. The entrance to parking at the city offices is on the right.

The Shining Sea Bikeway follows the route of a former railroad line run by the New York, New Haven and Hartford Railroad Company, which ran service to New York and Boston from 1872 to 1965. After the railroad company discontinued service along the line, local residents Joan Kanwisher, Barbara Burwell (mother of Rails-to-Trails Conservancy's cofounder David Burwell), and several other supporters organized in a nine-year-long effort to have the village of Woods Hole acquire the land and build a trail, which officially opened in June 1974.

It's no wonder that the bikeway was named after the lyrics to "America the Beautiful," written by Falmouth native Katharine Lee Bates. The 10.7-mile Shining Sea Bikeway—the only bikeway on Cape Cod to feature a seaside section—boasts beautiful vistas of marshes, rivers, and the sea.

The Shining Sea Bikeway boasts lovely vistas of marshes, rivers, and the sea.

County
Barnstable

Endpoints
County Road between Depot Road and MA 28A/N. Falmouth Hwy. (Falmouth) to Luscombe Ave. at Railroad Ave. (Woods Hole)

Mileage
10.7

Type
Rail-Trail/Rail-with-Trail

Roughness Index
1

Surface
Asphalt

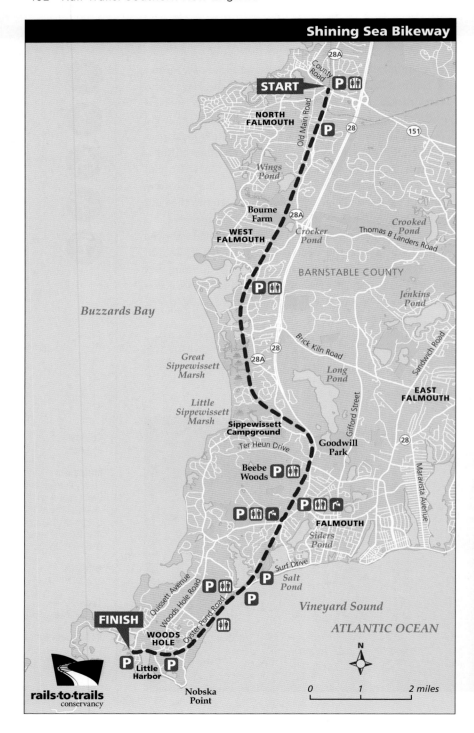

Near the southern end of the bikeway, stop to admire the ocean or even hit the water at Surf Drive Beach.

Although parking is available on either end of the trail, you'll want to start your journey at the Depot Road trailhead along County Road in Falmouth, as the scenic payoff for your efforts is located at the southern endpoint in Woods Hole. Turn left out of the parking lot on Depot Road (across from Pine Street), and use the sidewalk to travel 150 feet before using the crosswalk to enter the trail on the opposite side.

Along this stretch of trail, you can see railroad ties to your left—a nod to the trail's railroad history. After crossing Winslow Road in 0.6 mile, the path enters a wooded area and goes through an underpass decorated with bike-themed murals from the AmeriCorps Cape Cod program.

About 4 miles in, you will reach the Great Sippewissett Marsh on either side of the trail. The saltwater marsh is an important ecosystem habitat for the local flora and fauna. The Little Sippewissett Marsh is 1.3 miles farther ahead, and a connection to the Sippewissett Campground for backpackers is located on the left. The word Sippewissett, meaning "little river," comes from the Wampanoag tribe, the original inhabitants of the area.

The trail continues through a wooded area, with trailside businesses dotting the landscape. In 2 miles, as you near Depot Avenue/Highfield Drive in Falmouth, you will find plentiful parking in multiple lots. You will then pass a bus station on your left before crossing the road to enter another trailside parking lot. The trail continues into another wooded area (Beebe Woods), occasionally intersecting streets with light traffic.

At 8.5 miles into the trail, your hard work will be rewarded with stunning vistas of the Atlantic Ocean to the left as you pass by Surf Drive Beach. This makes for a perfect stopping point to rest and admire the ocean—or even take a dip in the water, as the swimming beach is fully accessible to visitors.

After leaving the unforgettable views of the ocean, you will pass through a final wooded section that belies its suburban neighborhood with the sound of cars passing on nearby roads and houses located on the left side of the trail. As you cross a short bridge and pass through a long, linear parking lot, take care, as from here to the end you may encounter cars along your route.

After crossing the Church Street overpass toward the end of the trail, you will find Little Harbor, docked with yachts, to your left. In 0.3 mile from Church Street, continue under the Crane Street overpass to reach the end of the trail. Friends of Falmouth Bikeways—and Friends of the Bourne Rail Trail—hope one day to extend the trail north to connect to the southern end of the Cape Cod Canal Bikeway (page 84) in Bourne.

CONTACT: friendsoffalmouthbikeways.org, capecodbikeguide.com/shiningsea.asp, and **falmouthmass.us/401/Bikeways-Committee**

DIRECTIONS

To reach the Depot Road trailhead in Falmouth from the intersection of US 6 and MA 28 in Buzzards Bay, head south on MA 28 for 7.6 miles, and take the exit for MA 151 toward Mashpee/N. Falmouth near mile marker 55. Turn left onto MA 151 W. Continue 0.5 mile and turn right into the Depot Road parking lot, located just after the train tracks and across from Pine St.

To reach the Woods Hole trailhead from the intersection of US 6 and MA 28 in Buzzards Bay, head south on MA 28 for 14.2 miles until Main St. in Falmouth curves to the right and becomes Locus St. In 0.3 mile bear right to continue on Woods Hole Road. Continue on Woods Hole Road 3.3 miles until Woods Hole Road becomes Water St. Turn left onto Luscombe Ave. and continue around the street until the entrance to the trail is visible, just past the new ferry ticket office as the trail travels under the Crane St. overpass. Metered street parking is available in and around the area, such as on Water St. and Luscombe Ave. A free parking lot is located along the interior of the trail between the Church St. and Nobska Road bridges that cross over the trail, though the first 45 numbered spots are reserved for residents. To reach the parking lot, you will need to drive on the trail from the Steamship Authority until you reach the lot. Watch out for trail users in all directions, as well as cars traveling in the opposite direction.

The Southwest Corridor Park (Pierre Lallement Bike Path) knits together neighborhoods in southern Boston from the Back Bay to Jamaica Plain. Popular as a route for commuters as well as casual walkers, runners, and cyclists, the 52-acre linear park passes skyscrapers, established residential areas, and community gardens.

The green space through the dense urban environment is a testament to residents who vociferously

Surrounded by parks, community gardens, and other recreational amenities, the trail winds through the southern neighborhoods of Boston.

County
Suffolk

Endpoints
Dartmouth St. between Stuart St. and Columbus Ave./MA 28 (Back Bay, Boston) to New Washington St. between South St. and Washington St. (Jamaica Plain, Boston)

Mileage
4.1

Type
Rail-with-Trail

Roughness Index
1

Surface
Asphalt

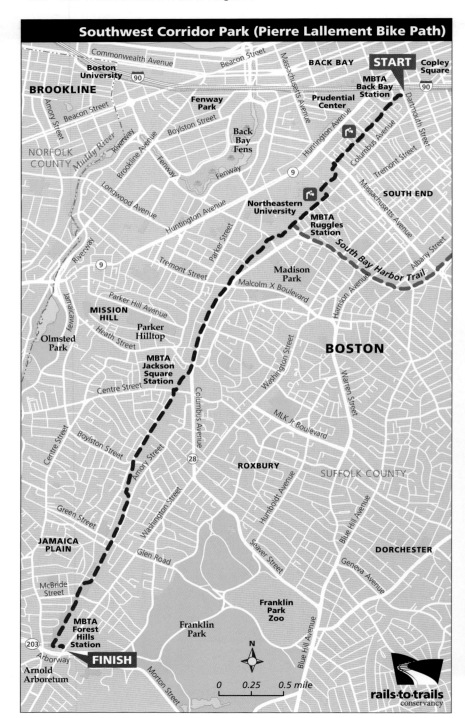

Southwest Corridor Park (Pierre Lallement Bike Path)

protested the bulldozing of their neighborhoods in the 1960s to make way for a 12-lane expressway. In the end, Governor Francis Sargent in 1969 discarded the highway plans for the razed corridor in favor of a 4.1-mile-long park featuring mass transit, open space, and recreation facilities.

Today, the Southwest Corridor Park parallels the Massachusetts Bay Transportation Authority's Orange Line, roughly following the old route of the Boston Elevated Railway built to Forest Hills in 1908. The Orange Line opened in 1987, and the city dedicated the park in 1990.

Along its length, the Southwest Corridor Park contains community gardens (maintained by Southwest Corridor Park Conservancy), playgrounds, basketball and tennis courts, spray pools, and trails, including a 4.1-mile bike path named for Pierre Lallement, credited as the inventor of the pedal bicycle in the 1860s. In some places, adjacent paths separate bicyclists and pedestrians.

The northern trailhead begins across from the south entrance of the Back Bay T station on Dartmouth Street, only blocks from Copley Square, the Boston Public Library, and commercial Newbury Street. The trail winds its way between small residential South End side streets lined with historical brownstones. This skillfully designed section includes dog parks, playgrounds, neighborhood vegetable gardens, and basketball and tennis courts.

As the trail crosses West Newton Street, you can see the Prudential Center and John Hancock buildings, landmarks on the Boston skyline. Symphony Hall, home to the Boston Symphony Orchestra, is a couple blocks north of the Massachusetts Avenue crossing as you enter Northeastern University's urban campus. Approaching the college's tennis courts, turn left and then right to remain on the path as it parallels Columbus Avenue for a short stretch to Ruggles Station, where you'll cross the 2-mile South Bay Harbor Trail. Scattered along the corridor are more tennis courts, basketball courts, spray pools, street hockey rinks, and amphitheaters.

The path continues along Columbus Avenue, then cuts behind Jackson Square Station, where murals line the corridor to Centre Street. You're never far from groceries and sandwich shops if you're hungry.

The trail ends just across Washington Street from Forest Hills Station, though you can extend your walk or ride into Arnold Arboretum, across South Street to the north of the station. The arboretum is part of landscape architect Frederick Law Olmsted's Emerald Necklace, a 1,100-acre chain of parks conceived in the 1870s for Boston and Brookline. It offers an alternate walking or bike route back downtown.

CONTACT: mass.gov/eea/agencies/dcr/massparks/region-boston/southwest -corridor-park.html and swcpc.org

DIRECTIONS

Driving is congested in Boston and parking is at a premium. Bicycles are allowed on MBTA commuter trains weekdays during off-peak hours and all day on weekends. Hubway bike share (**thehubway.com**) offers an alternative to taking your bike.

The northern trailhead is at the Back Bay T station on Dartmouth St., reachable on the Orange Line. To reach the trailhead from I-93, take Exit 18 toward Massachusetts Ave./Roxbury Frontage Road. From the exit ramp, head west on the Massachusetts Ave. Connector. In 0.3 mile turn right onto Massachusetts Ave., and go 1 mile. Turn right onto Avenue of the Arts/Huntington Ave., and go 0.5 mile, where the road becomes Stuart St. Turn right onto Dartmouth St. The trailhead is between MA 28/Columbus Ave. and Stuart St. Look for parking in the area.

The southern trailhead is at Forest Hills T station, also on the Orange Line. To reach the southern trailhead in Jamaica Plain from I-93, take Exit 2B toward MA 138/Milton. Go 1.1 miles north and veer right onto Canton Ave. Go 2.2 miles and turn left onto Blue Hills Pkwy. Go 2.7 miles and turn left onto MA 203/Morton St./Arborway. Go 1.8 miles and look for the trail on your right immediately after Washington St. Turn left onto Washington St. to find the Forest Hills T station parking.

Walkers and bicyclists alike enjoy Upper Charles Trail, a popular rail-trail crossing through small towns. Traveling the entirety of the trail puts users on varying trail surfaces, mostly packed cinder or asphalt—with both surfaces suitable for all bikes. While the route continues to be extended in length by local communities, the sections of trail approaching new endpoints may not have smooth surfaces.

Beginning in Holliston near Blair Square, the trail travels both north and south. The northern section of trail can be traversed to MA 16, a 1.3-mile distance, and will one day also extend another 1.5 miles beyond MA 16 (that section is currently very rough). For now, we recommend heading south from Blair Square, where the bulk of the trail continues.

The southern section of trail is completed and well maintained, heading out atop a packed cinder surface. Heading south on the trail, users will approach the historical Phipps Tunnel in about 1 mile. This tunnel was constructed to allow steam trains to travel under Highland

Travelers will have great opportunities to view wildlife in the adjacent forests and bogs.

Counties
Middlesex, Worcester

Endpoints
MA 16/Washington St. between Old Locust St. and Whitney St. (Holliston) to MA 85/Cedar St. across from Jacob Lane at Hopkinton town line (Milford)

Mileage
12.3

Type
Rail-Trail

Roughness Index
2

Surfaces
Asphalt, Ballast, Cinder

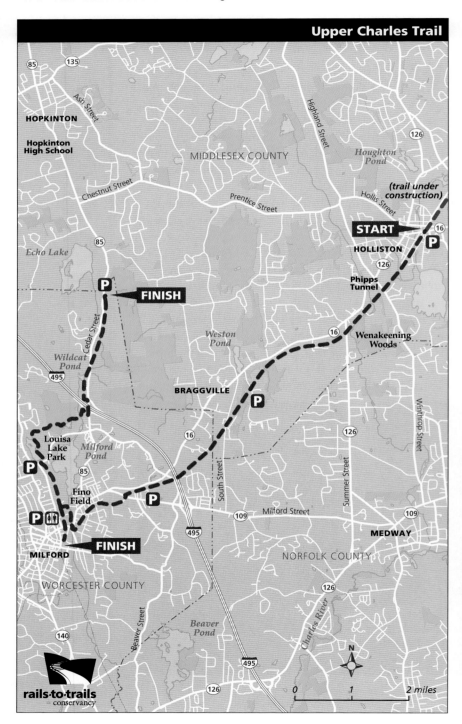

Upper Charles Trail

85 135

HOPKINTON

Ash Street

Hopkinton
High School

MIDDLESEX COUNTY

126

Highland Street

*Houghton
Pond*

Chestnut Street

Prentice Street

*(trail under
construction)*

Hollis Street

START   16
P

HOLLISTON

Echo Lake

85

126

Phipps
Tunnel

P
FINISH

Cedar Street

*Weston
Pond*

16

Wenakeening
Woods

*Wildcat
Pond*

495

BRAGGVILLE

P

Winthrop Street

Louisa
Lake
Park

*Milford
Pond*

16

126

P

85

Summer Street

Fino
Field

P

P

South Street

109   Milford Street

109

MEDWAY

FINISH

MILFORD

495

NORFOLK COUNTY

WORCESTER COUNTY

Beaver Street

*Beaver
Pond*

Charles River

126

N

140

126

495

0   1   2 miles

rails·to·trails
conservancy

Street—the design of the tunnel, with its curved walls, is quite unique. Throughout this stretch, it is clear how much the local community takes pride in the trail, from the clean and well-maintained surface to the installation of trailside art.

In another 2.8 miles, the path crosses South Street. About 5 miles into the trail, the surface transitions to asphalt, providing an opportunity for in-line skaters to also enjoy the trail. At this point, the path goes under the I-495/Blue Star Memorial Highway overpass. Several parking areas exist along the trail, providing opportunities for walkers, bicyclists, and skaters to enter the trail on either cinder or asphalt surface. Continuing another 1.6 miles puts users into the heart of Milford, where the trail makes several sharp bends before splitting at Fino Field (a municipal park facility maintained by the town of Milford). Bathrooms and parking are available here.

From Fino Field, you can turn left to go south about 0.2 mile before the trail stops, or turn right to head north, following the trail to its Hopkinton–Milford endpoint in 3.6 miles. Traveling north from this point provides trail users great opportunities to view wildlife in the adjacent forests and bogs, as well as alongside Milford Pond to the right and Louisa Lake Park to the left (0.9 mile from Fino Field). This stretch of trail includes several well-marked road crossings, designed for bicycle and pedestrian crossing. From Louisa Lake Park, the trail continues about 3 miles to public parking along Cedar Street in Milford.

CONTACT: uppercharlestrail.org

DIRECTIONS

To reach the eastern trailhead parking lot in Holliston from I-495, take Exit 19 for MA 109 toward Milford/Medway. Head east on MA 109 E/Medway Road. Go 0.5 mile, then turn left onto Clark St., which becomes South St. In 1.8 miles, turn right onto MA 16 E, and go 3 miles. Turn right onto Central St. in Holliston. Here, parking is available at Blair Square off Front St. and in a municipal parking lot off Exchange St.

To reach parking at Fino Field in Milford from I-495, take Exit 20 for MA 85 toward Milford/Hopkinton. Head south on MA 85 S/Cedar St. In 0.4 mile, turn right onto Dilla St. In 0.9 mile, turn left onto Sumner St. Fino Field will come up in 0.7 mile on the left. Parking is available off Granite St.

To reach parking at Louisa Lake Park in Milford from I-495, take Exit 20 for MA 85 toward Milford/Hopkinton. Head south on MA 85 S/Cedar St. In 0.2 mile, turn right onto Dilla St. Parking is available in 0.5 mile at Louisa Lake Park off Dilla St.

To reach the western trailhead parking lot in Hopkinton–Milford from I-495, take Exit 20 for MA 85 toward Milford/Hopkinton. Head north on MA 85 N/Cedar St. In 1.5 miles, just after passing Jacob Lane to your left, turn right off MA 85 N/Cedar St. A large parking lot is located here on Cedar St. at the Hopkinton town line.

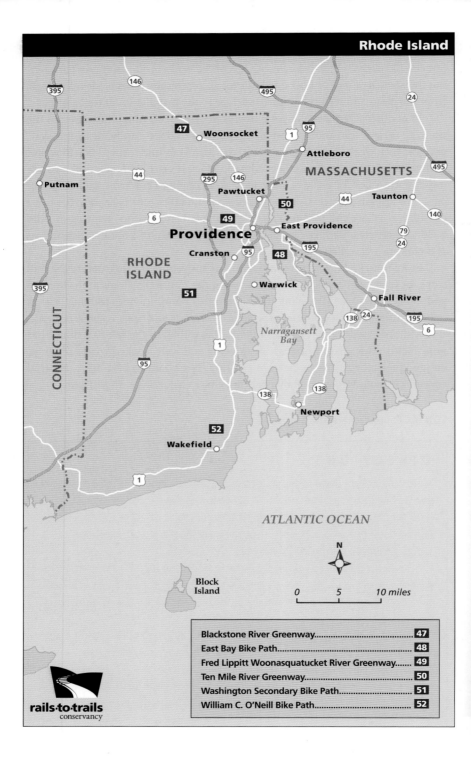

MASSACHUSETTS

146
395
495
24
47 Woonsocket
1
95
Attleboro
44
295 146
Putnam
Pawtucket
44
Taunton
140
6
50
49
East Providence
79
Providence
24
Cranston
95
48
195
RHODE
ISLAND
395
Warwick
51
Fall River
138
24
195
6
138
1
Narragansett
Bay
95
138
138
Newport
52
Wakefield
1

CONNECTICUT

ATLANTIC OCEAN

N

Block
Island

0   5   10 miles

rails·to·trails
conservancy

Rhode Island

Along the Fred Lippitt Woonasquatucket River Greenway (see page 182), you can see remnants of Providence's rich industrial history.

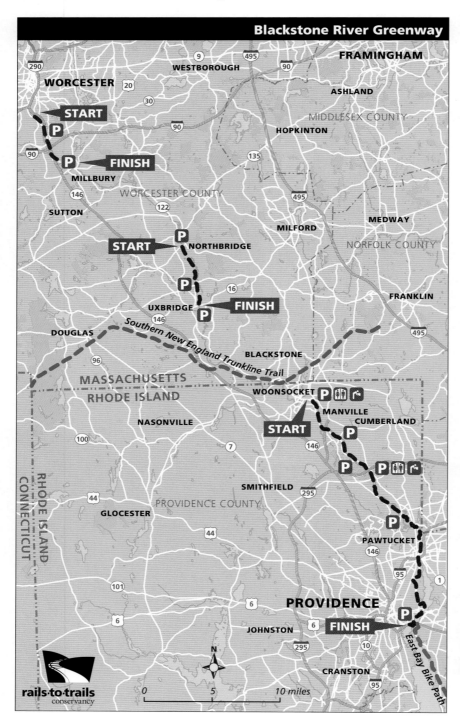

Throughout history, the Blackstone River has been an important waterway, from its use by American Indians who fished its once-abundant salmon to its role as a major artery for the transportation of raw materials and manufactured goods along its canal and riverways. Its widespread use during the Industrial Revolution earned it a reputation as "the hardest-working river" in America, though that legacy came at a cost, as the river would later be regarded as one of the most polluted in the country. The cleanup of the river is ongoing—and communities along its banks are embracing tourism and recreation as new industries, with the Blackstone River Greenway (also known as the Blackstone River Bikeway) as a major draw. The greenway is envisioned as a 50-mile network of trails and pathways along the riverbanks from Worcester, Massachusetts, to Providence, Rhode Island.

In Massachusetts completed off-road sections include a 3.5-mile segment that begins in South Worcester and ends in Millbury, and a tranquil 3.6-mile canalway in Blackstone River and Canal Heritage State Park. Currently, the longest off-road segment connects Woonsocket and Pawtucket in Rhode Island.

Counties
Worcester (MA),
Providence (RI)

Endpoints
McKeon Road, just east of Blackstone River Road (South Worcester, MA), to N. Main St. and MA 122A/Canal St. (Millbury, MA); Church St. and Commerce Dr. (Northbridge, MA) to Cross St. and Bruce St. (Uxbridge, MA); Davison Ave., just northeast of Manville Road/RI 126 (Woonsocket, RI), to Jones St. and Silva St. (Valley Falls, RI)

Mileage
26.6

Type
Rail-Trail/Canal/Rail-with-Trail

Roughness Index
1

Surfaces
Asphalt, Boardwalk, Crushed Stone, Dirt

The majestic George Washington Highway rises above the trail northwest of Pawtucket.

Just north of the Massachusetts–Rhode Island state line, the trail will one day connect to the Southern New England Trunkline Trail. On the southern end of the trail, you can continue on bike lanes and shared roadways into Providence, where you can connect to the East Bay Bike Path (see page 179) in India Point Park.

Visit the Blackstone Heritage Corridor website for greenway updates and maps with suggested on-road routes that connect the off-road trails.

South Worcester to Millbury (Massachusetts)

This 3.5-mile section begins at the Blackstone Heritage Corridor Visitor Center, where McKeon Road crosses Middle River.

The paved pathway heads south into Millbury, passing a railroad and winding under busy highways as it offers serene river views under a pleasant tree-lined canopy. A parking lot at Millbury Street has maps and information placards, a bike repair station, and bike racks. As you continue south, you'll see several forks that connect to nearby roadways—stay to the right to continue along the main trail.

The most picturesque portion is the trail's last 2 miles on its south end. Here, a small bridge carries you to the other side of the Blackstone River. Shortly after, the railroad makes an appearance again as you cross an intersecting branch of the river, revealing an interesting side-by-side view of a rail-with-trail. The trail continues to follow the railroad as you move toward the center of Millbury. One last underpass and a bend in the trail put you along Main Street and back across the river. The trail follows Main Street and ends at a small parking lot just off the road.

Blackstone River and Canal Heritage State Park (Massachusetts)

The 1,000-acre Blackstone River and Canal Heritage State Park offers a series of connecting, multiuse trails totaling 3.6 miles that wind through a lushly wooded corridor, mostly along the historical canal towpath. The park allows equestrians, in addition to walkers and cyclists, to enjoy the scenic setting.

The natural-surface trail begins at the Plummer's Landing trailhead on Church Street in Northbridge. From there, you'll follow the Plummer's Trail to the Canal Towpath, then take the Goat Hill Trail at Goat Hill Lock and continue south. Along the way, you'll find picnic tables, kayak and canoe access points, and opportunities for fishing and viewing wildlife.

Be sure to visit the River Bend Farm Visitor Center for exhibits on the history of the canal and more information about the Blackstone River corridor. The trail ends 0.75 mile later at the restored 19th-century Stanley Woolen Mill on Cross Street in Uxbridge.

Woonsocket to Providence (Rhode Island)

The Blackstone River Greenway in Rhode Island spans 19.5 miles, including some on-road riding. The paved pathway begins at the Rivers Edge Parking Area on the western bank of the Blackstone River in Woonsocket, a city that borders the Massachusetts–Rhode Island state line. From the trailhead, you'll travel south through the heart of the river's industrial past.

The trail is fairly wide with excellent wayfinding signage. After briefly following along a park access road, the trail crosses the road and continues through the Rivers Edge Recreation Complex, where you'll have access to putting greens, a playground, restroom facilities, and multiple sports fields. Traveling out of the park, the trail parallels an active rail line as you make your way south, leaving Woonsocket behind and entering the community of Manville. There are multiple places to stop along the way to take in the beauty of the river and read interpretive signage about the trail's history.

Eventually, the rail-with-trail crosses the Blackstone River, allowing for an unusual view of this side-by-side configuration of trail and rail over the water. Now on the other side of the river, the trail snakes down and under I-295, which surrounds Providence. The path crosses over the Blackstone River at the impressive Ashton Mill. Once producing cotton fabrics, this vast industrial complex has been converted into riverside apartments and lofts. The Ashton Mill and its surrounding homes were one of four mill villages that lined the river in this area—built and owned by the Lonsdale Company in the 19th century. Here, you'll also pass the Captain Wilbur Kelly House Museum. Housed in the historical residence of a canalboat captain, the museum displays the history of transportation along the Blackstone River and canal, from prehistory through the Industrial Revolution.

You can roll or stroll along portions of the crushed-stone canalway that intersect the paved rail-trail. A branch of the trail also heads north to the large Blackstone Valley Visitor Center, off I-295. In addition to drinking water and restrooms, the center has a gift shop, a gallery, and exhibits about the Blackstone Valley river corridor. Don't miss the vast terrazzo floor map of the valley, complete with the Blackstone River Greenway.

Head south of the Kelly House Museum on the main trail and you'll pass under the Martin Street bridge, with its striking timber bowstring trusses. After 1.5 miles, you'll arrive in Lonsdale, one of the mill villages along the banks of the Blackstone River. To the east, you'll find a short pathway to parking near Lonsdale Mill. Cross over the churning Pratt Dam on an impressive bridge that uses the original stone piers from the trail's railway past. About a mile away, you'll come to another parking area—this one is marked with a restored drive-in theater sign, featuring the Blackstone River Bikeway and habitat restoration on its marquis. The trail meanders through secluded marshland over a boardwalk bridge, where it comes to an end at Jones Street.

Signs continue for a section of on-street bikeway to reach the Valley Falls Heritage Park in Pawtucket. You can continue on-road to just under the I-95 overpass on Taft Street, where spacious bike lanes and sharrows (symbols indicating a shared bike-vehicle lane) lead the way. Take a right onto Bowles Street, then a left onto Pleasant Street. You'll veer right onto Alfred Stone Road and cross Blackstone Boulevard onto a tree-lined pathway for about 1.6 miles. Turn left onto Irving Avenue, then right onto River Road for a pleasant ride along the banks of the Seekonk River to the end of your journey. In India Point Park, you can pick up the East Bay Bike Path, which heads southeast for just over 14 miles to Bristol.

CONTACT: blackstoneheritagecorridor.org/exploring-the-blackstone-river-valley /maps-tours-guides/blackstone-river-bikeway

DIRECTIONS

Northernmost access in Worcester: Parking will be available at the Blackstone Heritage Corridor Visitor Center off McKeon Road in Worcester. At press time, the northernmost parking lot for the trail can be found just south of the intersection of Millbury and Cliff Sts. in Worcester. From I-90 (Massachusetts Turnpike), take Exit 10A toward US 20/MA 146. At the end of the exit ramp, turn right to merge onto MA 122A/MA 146. In 0.6 mile exit and turn right onto Millbury St. Drive south 0.4 mile to Cliff St. The trail parking lot will appear on your right.

Blackstone River and Canal Heritage State Park: To reach the River Bend Farm Visitor Center from I-90, take Exit 10A toward Worcester/Providence. At the end of the exit ramp, turn right, then turn right again onto MA 146 S toward Millbury/Providence. Merge onto MA 146 S, and continue 12.1 mile. Take Exit 3 for MA 16 toward Uxbridge/Douglas, then turn left onto MA 16/Douglas St. After 2.3 miles, turn right onto MA 16/MA 122. Take the next left onto MA 16/ Mendon St. In 0.3 mile turn left onto Oak St., and the entrance to the state park will be on your right in 1.1 miles.

Woonsocket: To reach the Rivers Edge Parking Area on Davison Ave. in Woonsocket from I-295, take Exit 9B for RI 146 N toward Woonsocket, then in 0.3 mile take the exit for RI 99 N. In 2.8 miles, turn left onto RI 122/Mendon Road toward Woonsocket. In 1.5 miles, turn left onto Hamlet Ave. Just after crossing the river, turn left onto Davison Ave. The parking lot will be on your left, just past the Veterans Memorial. The trail begins at the south end of the parking lot.

Lonsdale: To reach the parking area and trail access point near the Pratt Dam in Lonsdale from I-295, take Exit 10 for RI 122 toward Cumberland. Turn left onto RI 122/Mendon Road. In 3.25 miles, turn right onto RI 123/Front St. After a slight bend in the road, in 0.2 mile, turn right into the entrance of Blackstone River State Park.

Numerous points along the trail offer parking and access. Visit the website above or **TrailLink.com** for detailed maps and driving directions for those locations.

With spectacular maritime views and an abundance of coastal wildlife, the East Bay Bike Path offers a spectacular New England experience. Inducted into the Rail-Trail Hall of Fame in 2009, the route is one of the most popular multiuse trails in Rhode Island. The paved pathway travels just over 14 miles between Providence and Bristol, visiting eight parks as it skirts the historical waterfronts that played roles in local shipbuilding, transoceanic trade, and manufacturing.

The rail-trail follows a railbed whose various owners helped shape East Coast railroads over a century. The Providence, Warren and Bristol Railroad completed the line in 1855. The Old Colony Railroad leased it beginning in 1891, but it soon came under control of the New York, New Haven and Hartford Railroad (the New Haven). Penn Central acquired the New Haven in 1969 and discontinued the Bristol-Providence line in 1973. The state built most of the bike trail between 1987 and 1992.

The George Redman Linear Park over the Seekonk River was named for a leading advocate of the trail.

Counties
Bristol, Providence

Endpoints
Tockwotton St. and India St. at India Point Park (Providence) to Thames St. and Oliver St. in Independence Park (Bristol)

Mileage
14.3

Type
Rail-Trail

Roughness Index
1

Surface
Asphalt

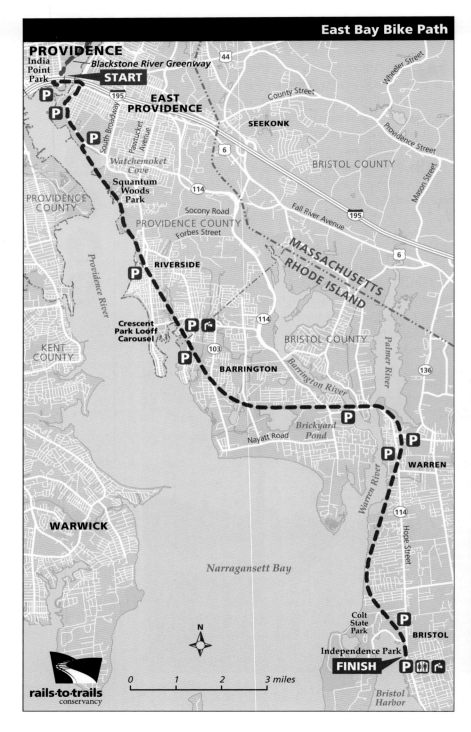

East Bay Bike Path

PROVIDENCE
India Point Park
Blackstone River Greenway
START
EAST PROVIDENCE
SEEKONK
County Street
Wheeler Street
Providence Street
Mason Street
BRISTOL COUNTY
Watchemoket Cove
Squantum Woods Park
PROVIDENCE COUNTY
Socony Road
Forbes Street
Fall River Avenue
MASSACHUSETTS
RHODE ISLAND
RIVERSIDE
Providence River
Crescent Park Looff Carousel
KENT COUNTY
BARRINGTON
BRISTOL COUNTY
Palmer River
Brickyard Pond
Nayatt Road
Barrington River
Warren River
WARREN
Hope Street
WARWICK
Narragansett Bay
Colt State Park
BRISTOL
Independence Park
FINISH
Bristol Harbor

N

0   1   2   3 miles

rails·to·trails
conservancy

India Point Park is a good place to embark on a journey on the East Bay Bike Path. The trail follows a ramp up to a pedestrian bridge named George Redman Linear Park, memorializing a local bike advocate. The bridge reopened in 2015 after serving since the 1930s as the eastbound span of the Washington Bridge.

Arriving in East Providence, you'll head south on First Street for two blocks before regaining the trail, which is separated from Victory Parkway by a split rail fence for the next 1.1 miles. You'll drop down a steep embankment to the old railroad corridor spanning Watchemoket Cove on a causeway, where the railroad was double-tracked and the other set of tracks is often visible. You'll have unobstructed views of the Providence skyline and shipping facilities from here and up ahead at Squantum Woods Park, where some 90 bird species have been recorded.

The next mile is wooded before you reach the Riverside community. You'll recognize an old railroad station just before Lincoln Avenue, and in another mile you'll cross Crescent View Avenue. Here you can turn right on a 0.5-mile side trip to the Crescent Park Looff Carousel, an 1895 amusement ride that features 62 carved figures and four chariots. It's listed on the National Register of Historic Places.

The trail veers away from the bay for 6 miles as it passes through Barrington; the bridges crossing Barrington and Palmer Rivers are popular fishing spots. Commercial districts in Riverside, Barrington, and up ahead in Warren and Bristol all offer opportunities for snacks and refreshments. The trail ends along Bristol Harbor, just past the entrance to Colt State Park.

The stature of the East Bay Bike Path, one of the longest trails in the state, will grow with a connection to the developing Blackstone River Greenway (see page 174), which extends into Massachusetts. The bike path is also a part of the East Coast Greenway, a growing trail network between Maine and Florida.

CONTACT: riparks.com/locations/locationeastbay.html

DIRECTIONS

To reach the Providence trailhead, take I-95 to Exit 19 and merge onto I-195 E. Take Exit 2 for India St. to Gano St. Turn left into India Point Park. The trailhead is on the right; ramps lead up to the bridge where the path begins as a separated corridor alongside traffic.

There are many other places to park along the trail. The closest parking lots to the northern terminus are on Veterans Memorial Pkwy. in East Providence. Traveling east on I-195 from Providence, take Exit 4 to Riverside. Merge onto Veterans Memorial Pkwy., and in 0.3 mile, near Mercer St., you'll find two parking lots on the right.

To reach the Colt State Park trailhead in Bristol, take I-195 E into Massachusetts and take Exit 2. Follow MA 136 S 1.2 miles to Rhode Island, and continue on RI 136 S another 2.5 miles. Turn right onto Vernon St. in Warren, and then in 0.6 mile, turn left onto RI 114 S and go 2.3 miles toward Bristol. In Bristol, turn right onto Asylum Road and go 0.5 mile.

Fred Lippitt Woonasquatucket River Greenway

The Fred Lippitt Woonasquatucket River Greenway provides a valuable crosstown connector of nearly 7 miles from downtown Providence to the city's western neighborhoods and the nearby town of Johnston. In addition to being named for the river it parallels, the greenway honors a Rhode Island politician and philanthropist who championed the project in the early 1990s as a means to revitalize some of Providence's poorest and most underserved neighborhoods.

The rail-trail follows the route of the Providence & Springfield Railroad, which was built in 1873 to service the mill villages along the river. Around the turn of the 19th century, the line was acquired by the New York, New Haven and Hartford Railroad, but it fell into disuse by the 1960s.

While the trail's eastern half is a patchwork of on-road bike routes and off-road pathways, its western half, beginning at Riverside Park, consists entirely of paved trail.

This vibrant mural can be found just east of Riverside Park.

County
Providence

Endpoints
Finance Way and Francis St. (Providence) to the dead end of Lyman Ave., 0.2 mile east of Greenville Ave. (Johnston)

Mileage
6.8

Type
Rail-Trail

Roughness Index
1

Surface
Asphalt

This artwork in Riverside Park illustrates the wildlife you might see along the trail.

Before you set out on your journey, note that the trail lacks restrooms or drinking water, so plan accordingly.

Riverside Park makes a great launching point, with a parking lot, large playground, and signage about the local wildlife, such as great blue herons, great white egrets, and marsh wrens. Moments after starting your trip on the trail's western leg, you'll pass an observation platform in the park with a view of the Woonasquatucket River. Continuing on the path, you'll head northwest past picnic tables, a self-service bike repair station, and swaths of wildflowers. At the end of the park, the trail splits; stay right to continue on the main pathway or veer left to cross a pedestrian bridge over US 6 into Merino Park, which has another playground and athletic fields. Although you'll parallel the highway a short distance, the tree-filled stream valley between you and traffic keeps the experience pleasant.

Upon completing the first mile, you'll see a spur off to your right that provides access to Manton Gateway Skate Park and Manton Avenue beyond. A little farther on, you'll be presented with another opportunity to veer off the trail and loop around the Button Hole Golf Course; otherwise, you can continue straight ahead. At the intersection of Greenville and Traver Avenues, you pop out of the lush greenery and enter a bustling area with a couple of restaurants nearby before crossing the street and heading back into the brush. From here, it's less than a mile to trail's end; you'll continue through woodlands, but homes and industry become noticeable just beyond the trees. The path stops at a dead end for Lyman Avenue in the heart of a residential neighborhood in Johnston. There's trail signage here but no parking.

To explore the eastern half of the trail, Riverside Park is also an optimal starting point. From the park entrance, you'll turn right onto Aleppo Street, followed by another right at the very next intersection, which is Manton Avenue. Along Manton, you'll pass an eye-catching redbrick industrial space, which was once a worsted mill; today it's home to a flea market and furniture store. In two blocks, turn left onto Delaine Street. After 0.2 mile, you'll turn left onto Sonoma Court, which quickly dead-ends into paved trail, where you'll be greeted with a vibrant mural.

Back on the pathway, you'll pedal past Rising Sun Mills, another monument to Providence's rich industrial history. Although the mill has been converted into commercial space and loft apartments, you can take a quick side trip here to see the remnants of the dam and water control mechanism that once powered the mill, as well as view a fish ladder that allows migratory fish to bypass the dam and move freely between Narragansett Bay and the Woonasquatucket River watershed. This section continues through the adjacent Donigian Park to its end at Valley Street, a total of 0.3 mile of paved-trail riding. East of Donigian Park, the route will be mostly on-road to the end of the line, another 1.5 miles.

After crossing Valley Street, continue straight onto Amherst Street, which you'll travel on for just one block before turning left onto Tuxedo Avenue. In another block, you'll come to Atwells Avenue; cross the street and you'll see the entrance to another section of paved trail on the other side of the crosswalk. This section of paved trail lasts 0.2 mile, ending at Eagle Street. At the intersection to your right, hop on the marked on-road bike lane along Kinsley Avenue, which heads northeast. The sparsely trafficked avenue becomes Providence Place closer to downtown.

As you approach trail's end, you'll see the elevated portions of I-95 overhead, and rising just beyond that, Providence Place, the largest mall in the state. An intriguing path will take you under the mall, alongside the Woonasquatucket River (which the building straddles), and over Amtrak Northeast Corridor rails that service nearby Providence Station.

The route officially ends as you emerge on the other side of the mall; there's a bike rack here and it's worth taking some time to enjoy the shopping and restaurants that the mall has to offer. Less than 0.25 mile north is the state capitol, and just across the street and down some steps is vibrant Waterplace Park, a lovely riverfront walk with public art, outdoor concert space, and more places to eat—the perfect ending to your biking adventure.

CONTACT: woonasquatucket.org/greenway.php and dot.ri.gov/community /bikeri/woonasquatucket.php

DIRECTIONS

Parking is available at Riverside Park (50 Aleppo St., Providence), roughly the midpoint of the trail. From downtown Providence, take Memorial Blvd. west to US 6 W (Huntington Expwy.). After 1.1 miles, stay right to continue on US 6. In another 0.5 mile, take the Hartford Ave. exit. At the fork, veer right and then turn right onto Hartford Ave. In just over 300 feet, turn right onto Atwood St. Take the very next left onto Plainfield St. and travel 0.1 mile to a left turn onto Manton Ave. Continue on Manton 0.2 mile until you reach a fork in the road; veer left at the fork onto Aleppo St. In less than 500 feet, you'll see Riverside Park and the entrance to the trail on your left.

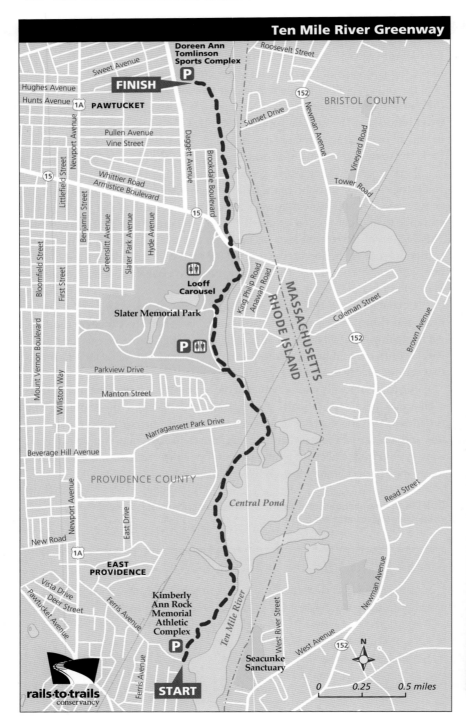

Ten Mile River Greenway

Ten Mile River Greenway, named for the waterway it parallels and not its length, runs 3 miles through a serene and green corridor connecting the City of East Providence and Pawtucket. The southern end of the paved pathway begins at the Kimberly Ann Rock Memorial Athletic Complex, a popular spot for local sporting events, where you'll find a large parking lot flanked by trees. If a game is playing when you arrive, restrooms will be available, but the bathrooms are otherwise locked, so they are not marked on the trail map. The trail also does not offer any drinking fountains, so be sure to pack water.

The greenway heads north, loosely paralleling the state's border with Massachusetts, and winds through leafy woodlands with an occasional pine tree. To your right, the adjacent river glimmers through the leaves. At intermittent spots along the trail, you can hop off your bike and walk

The tree-canopied trail truly feels like a "greenway."

County
Providence

Endpoints
Kimberly Ann Rock Memorial Athletic Complex (220 Ferris Ave.) (East Providence) and Doreen Ann Tomlinson Sports Complex, at the intersection of Daggett Ave. and Hutchinson Ave. (Pawtucket)

Mileage
3.0

Type
Greenway/Non-Rail-Trail

Roughness Index
1

Surface
Asphalt

The path parallels the Ten Mile River, where travelers are likely to see swans and other birds.

down to the waterfront, where you might see swans gliding through the calm water. Interpretative signage about the area's flora and fauna can be found trailside.

As you near the 2-mile mark, you'll approach Slater Memorial Park on the left, with a large parking lot, picnic tables, and portable toilets. As you continue forward, keep your eyes peeled for a tan building just off the trail to the left; you won't want to miss it, as it houses a beautiful Looff Carousel built in 1895. In addition to leaping horses with bejeweled saddles, it offers lions, dogs, and a giraffe to ride. Inside you can buy tickets, snacks, and cold drinks. At the nearby boathouse on the banks of a large pond, you can also rent swan- and dragon-shaped paddle-boats to enjoy on the water.

A little farther on is the trail's only street crossing at Armistice Boulevard. Beyond it, the last mile of the trail has a few gentle climbs and curves that vary the experience. The pathway ends as it began, at a large parking lot, this one for the Doreen Ann Tomlinson Sports Complex.

CONTACT: dot.ri.gov/community/bikeri/tenmile.php

DIRECTIONS

To get to East Providence's Kimberly Ann Rock Memorial Athletic Complex at the southern end of the trail, take I-195 E to Exit 4 to US 44/Taunton Ave. Take Taunton 0.8 mile; it becomes Waterman Ave. Cross S. Broadway then bear left onto Hall St. and in 0.1 mile bear right onto Taunton Ave. Continue 0.4 mile to the intersection with Pawtucket Ave. and turn left (RI 114/US 1A). In 1.5 miles, at the intersection with Newman Ave. and Ferris Ave., bear right onto Ferris; the sign for the Ten Mile River Greenway parking is about 0.5 mile on the right.

To get to Pawtucket's Doreen Ann Tomlinson Sports Complex at the northern end of the trail, take I-95 N to Exit 29 (Cottage St.). Turn left onto Cottage St., and in 0.3 mile bear right onto Central Ave. In 1.3 miles turn right onto Daggett Ave., and in 0.3 mile take a left at the baseball field to enter the parking lot.

The Washington Secondary Bike Path offers just over 19 miles of paved trail from Cranston (Providence's southwestern neighbor) to Coventry. The rail-trail, Rhode Island's longest, follows the former Hartford, Providence and Fishkill Railroad. Although sections of the trail have their own distinct local names—Cranston Bike Path, Warwick Bike Path, West Warwick Greenway, Coventry Greenway, and Trestle Trail—the overall experience is seamless. The trail is also part of the expansive and developing East Coast Greenway, which connects paths throughout New England and all the way down to Florida.

Locals will tell you that the farther west you travel on the trail, the prettier it gets; their advice rings true, so a

Several beautiful bridges dot the west end of the trail in Coventry.

Counties
Kent, Providence

Endpoints
Dead end of Depot Ave., near its intersection with Cory Ave. (Cranston), to Railroad St. and Log Bridge Road (Coventry)

Mileage
19.2

Type
Rail-Trail

Roughness Index
1

Surface
Asphalt

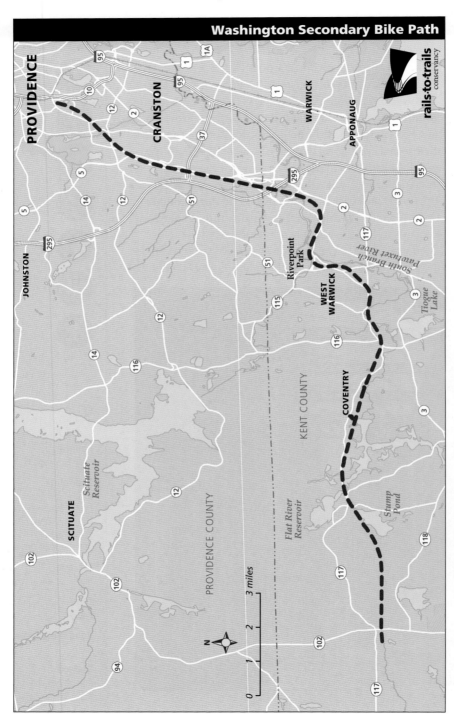

nice place to begin your journey is in the middle and then head west for a well-shaded and scenic ride. (You could also start at the west end and ride toward the middle to enjoy a slight downhill grade.) This western half has a rural feel to it and includes a parallel bridle path.

The eastern half of the trail is more urban in flavor with residential and commercial areas pressed close alongside. This Cranston end of the trail is not as well maintained, and though it serves as a useful route for residents, tourists may not find it as appealing.

A good mid-route starting point is the trail parking lot adjacent to Horgan Elementary School in West Warwick. (Riverpoint Park, also located in this area but a touch farther from the trail, is another option.) Be sure to take a moment to check out the bright-red New York, New Haven and Hartford Railroad caboose on display at the east end of the school complex; while it's only 200 feet from the path, the sight lines are such that it can be easy to miss. Once on the path, head southwest, wending through the heart of West Warwick. From here to the west end of the trail is an 11-mile ride.

Although numerous street crossings occur along this section, each is well marked and most are across smaller secondary roads with little traffic. These crossings also provide a convenient way to step off the trail and grab a bite to eat or hit a restroom—useful options since there are few amenities along the trail itself.

As you enter Coventry, you'll find yourself sharing the trail with bikers, joggers, dog walkers, families with young children, and leisurely amblers—and it's no wonder that the trail is so popular, as it's smoothly paved and surrounded by tall trees. The nearby Pawtuxet River has a sinuous route, so you'll cross it a couple of times on beautiful bridges with nice views.

As you traverse Coventry, look for a short section of preserved railroad track that parallels the trail; a trailhead kiosk here provides information about the trail's history. Continuing west, you'll have views of Flat River Reservoir, a recreational hot spot for fishing and boating. Farther on, the trail travels through fern-covered rock cuts and the tree canopy gets thicker, for a cool, pleasant ride.

At Hill Farm Road, the route pops out of the trees into a more open area with a few houses and small businesses nearby. You'll find a large parking lot adjacent to the trail and more interpretive signage on railroad history. From here, it's only another 3.5 miles of riding to where the trail stops unceremoniously at a wall of brush. There's another large parking lot at trail's end, which is helpful if you've coordinated a pickup, and a general store with drinks and snacks to refuel.

Trail advocates hope to one day extend the trail another 6 miles west to the Connecticut border, where a connection to the Moosup Valley State Park Trail awaits.

A New York, New Haven and Hartford Railroad caboose is on display in West Warwick.

CONTACT: dot.ri.gov/community/bikeri/washington.php

DIRECTIONS

To start in West Warwick at the parking lot adjacent to Horgan Elementary School, from Providence, take I-95 S to Exit 12B for RI 113 W in Warwick (about 9 miles from the downtown area). Go 0.6 mile on RI 113 W, and turn left onto Bald Hill Road. In 0.7 mile, turn right onto Toll Gate Road. After 0.5 mile, veer left onto Providence St. In 0.8 mile, turn right onto Hay St. (You'll see the red caboose from the intersection and will be turning toward it.) Take an immediate left onto Junior St. and look for the entrance to the trail parking lot on your right. (The school will be on the opposite side of the street.)

To reach the west end of the trail in Coventry, take I-95 S from Providence to Exit 10B for RI 117 W. Take RI 117 westbound 2.6 miles, then turn right onto Main St. and make an immediate left onto Warwick Ave. to remain on RI 117. In 0.6 mile turn left onto Washington St./RI 117, and continue 9.9 miles to Old Summit Road, on which you'll turn left. The road becomes Log Bridge Road, and in 0.2 mile, you'll see the trail parking lot on your right.

Imagine a wealthy 19th-century textile mill owner building an 8-mile railroad to get coal to his plant or products to market, and then adding accommodations to carry vacationers to beach resorts or voyagers to steamships: that's the story of the short-line railroad that later became the William C. O'Neill Bike Path. At just over 7 miles, it runs from Amtrak's West Kingston Station to within about a mile of its original destination in the town of Narragansett Pier.

The paved rail-trail in southern Rhode Island is named for the late senator who spearheaded development of the trail, previously known as the South County Bike Path. (Washington County is locally known as South County.) It follows the railbed of the Narragansett Pier Railroad, opened in 1876 by a man who owned mills in Wakefield and Peace Dale. In 1921, rail buses—actual buses adapted to ride the rails—replaced the passenger cars. Locals affectionately called these unique buses Micky Dinks after two of the drivers. Passenger service ended in 1952, though freight service continued for another 25-plus years. The first section of the rail-trail opened in 2000.

The path offers an easy, paved route connecting the towns of West Kingston and Narragansett.

County
Washington

Endpoints
West Kingston Station at Railroad Ave. and Kingstown Road (West Kingston) to Mumford Road and Riverside Dr. (Narragansett)

Mileage
7.2

Type
Rail-Trail

Roughness Index
1

Surface
Asphalt

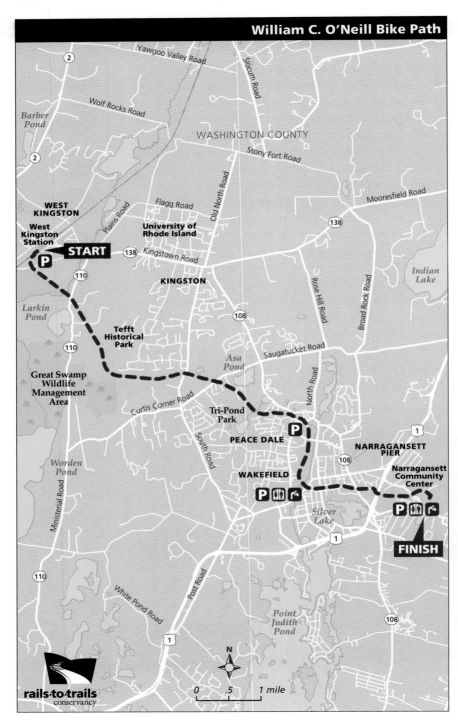

William C. O'Neill Bike Path

A good place to start is the Amtrak station in the West Kingston community. Built by the New York, Providence and Boston Railroad in 1874, the station was shared with the Narragansett Pier Railroad to transfer passengers heading to the beaches. You'll head south on the trail under a dense canopy of trees. Although you won't be able to see it from the pathway, the University of Rhode Island is nearby; as you approach your first mile on the trail, note that a connecting trail, scheduled for completion in late 2018 or 2019, will travel 2.1 miles to the campus.

This wooded area fringes the Great Swamp Wildlife Management Area, where, particularly in the spring and fall, you'll encounter flocks of migratory birds. Also in the woods is the Tefft Historical Park, where archaeological sites date from early Narragansett tribal occupation through Colonial settlements. At about mile 4, you'll enter the Tri-Pond Park, where you'll find ponds, streams, nature trails, and a nature center.

Emerging from the woods in Peace Dale (named for the railroad builder's mother), the trail takes Railroad Street for 0.2 mile. About midway on the left sits the renovated train depot, now a business. Crossing Church Street, you return to the trail. In 0.7 mile, you cross Main Street in Wakefield and see a replica train station. Arriving at the commercial center on Kingstown Road, the trail follows MacArthur Boulevard for 0.2 mile, then veers right back onto the trail.

The trail ends at Mumford Road, but across the street is a developing new section that's scheduled to open in late 2018 or early 2019. It will travel behind Narragansett Elementary School and end at the parking lot for the Narragansett Community Center. From here, another future segment will complete the journey to Narragansett Town Beach on the former right-of-way of Narragansett Pier Railroad's main rival, the Sea View Railroad.

CONTACT: southcountybikepath.org and dot.ri.gov/community/bikeri/southcounty.php

DIRECTIONS

To reach the trailhead at West Kingston Station, from I-95, take Exit 3A onto RI 138 E/Kingstown Road toward South Kingstown. Go 8.3 miles and turn right onto Railroad Ave.; you'll see signs for both the train station and the trail immediately before your turn. Go 0.1 mile and look for parking on the right. The trail starts at the southwest end of Railroad Ave.

To reach the trailhead at Narragansett, from US 1, take the exit for Wakefield. If on US 1 N, at the end of the exit ramp, the road ends in a T; turn right onto Narragansett Ave. E., which becomes Mumford Road. If on US 1 S, at the end of the exit ramp, turn left and then right onto Narragansett Ave. E., which becomes Mumford Road. Go 0.5 mile and turn left into the parking lot for the Narragansett Community Center (53 Mumford Road), which is adjacent to Narragansett Elementary School. To get to the trail, exit the parking lot, turn right and pass in front of the school, then turn right onto Mumford Road. Travel 0.2 mile to find the trail on your left.

Index

Photo Credits

Page iii: Jim Brown; *page vi:* Bill Cannon; *page ix:* Robert Bissell; *page x:* Milo Bateman; *page 7:* Yvonne Mwangi; *page 9:* Liz Sewell; *page 10:* Bob Youker; *page 13:* Jim Brown; *pages 14 and 17:* Eli Griffen; *page 19:* Bill Cannon; *page 23:* Liz Sewell; *page 27:* Bill Cannon; *page 29:* Yvonne Mwangi; *page 33:* John M. Joy; *pages 35 and 37:* Bill Cannon; *page 39:* Eli Griffen; *page 45:* Jim Brown; *pages 47 and 50:* Shoreline Greenway Trail, Inc.; *pages 51 and 55:* Yvonne Mwangi; *page 57:* Jim Brown; *page 61:* Anya Saretzky; *page 63:* Ron Fortier; *page 65:* Douglas Hurteau; *page 69:* Jing Zhou; *page 73:* Anya Saretzky; *pages 75 and 77:* David Alexander; *page 79:* Milo Bateman; *page 81:* Ken Bryan; *pages 85 and 86:* Anya Saretzky; *page 89:* Stephen Struble; *page 91:* Anya Saretzky; *page 95:* Georgie Vining; *page 99:* Milo Bateman; *page 103:* Leeann Sinpatanasakul; *pages 105 and 107:* Ken Bryan; *page 109:* Anya Saretzky; *page 113:* Ken Bryan; *page 115:* Andrew Riedl; *pages 119 and 120:* Milo Bateman; *page 125:* Andrew Riedl; *page 129:* Friends of Bedford Depot Park; *pages 131 and 133:* Milo Bateman; *page 135:* Leeann Sinpatanasakul; *page 139:* Ken Bryan; *page 143:* Leeann Sinpatanasakul; *pages 147 and 148:* Tom Sexton; *page 151:* John Charbonneau; *page 153:* Anya Saretzky; *page 157:* Aykut Bilge; *page 161:* Anya Saretzky; *page 163:* Leeann Sinpatanasakul; *page 165:* Jennifer Leonard; *page 169:* Ken Bryan; *page 173:* Scott Stark; *page 175:* Milo Bateman; *pages 179, 183, 184, 187, and 188:* Scott Stark; *page 189:* Laura Stark; *page 192:* Scott Stark; *page 193:* Kenneth C. Zirkel.

Support Rails-to-Trails Conservancy

The nation's leader in helping communities transform unused rail lines and connecting corridors into multiuse trails, Rails-to-Trails Conservancy (RTC) depends on the support of its members and donors to create access to healthy outdoor experiences.

Your donation will help support programs and services that have helped put more than 23,000 rail-trail miles on the ground. Every day, RTC provides vital assistance to communities to develop and maintain trails throughout the country. In addition, RTC advocates for trail-friendly policies, promotes the benefits of rail-trails, and defends rail-trail laws in the courts.

Join online at railstotrails.org, or mail your donation to Rails-to-Trails Conservancy, 2121 Ward Court NW, Fifth Floor, Washington, D.C. 20037.

Rails-to-Trails Conservancy is a 501(c)(3) nonprofit organization, and contributions are tax deductible.